SMOOTH GUIDE TO YORKSHIRE GALLERIES

Smooth Guide to Yorkshire Galleries

Mary Sara

Smith
Settle

First published in 1992 by
Smith Settle Ltd
Ilkley Road
Otley
West Yorkshire   LS21 3JP

© Mary Sara 1992
Illustrations © The Contributors 1992

ISBN 1 870071 90 5

British Library Cataloguing-in-Publication Data:
A catalogue record for this book is available from the British
Library

Frontispiece: *sizing up Anthony Gormley's* Untitled *(1980) in
'Inside/Out: the gallery through young people's eyes' at Leeds
City Art Gallery.*

*Whilst every effort has been made to ensure the accuracy of
the information within this book, neither the publishers nor the
author accept responsibility for any changes that may have
occurred since this book was compiled.*

Designed, printed and bound by
SMITH SETTLE
Ilkley Road Otley West Yorkshire LS21 3JP

CONTENTS

ACKNOWLEDGEMENTS

1853 Gallery, Saltaire, p7; Barnsley MBC: Dept of Leisure & Amenities, p62, 63; Booth House Gallery, Holmfirth, p51; Bradford Art Galleries and Museums, p2, 4, 5, 17 (photo: Philip Bambridge); Calderdale Leisure Services, p40 (photo: Barry Wood Ltd), 46; Cliffe Castle Museum, Keighley, p19; Craft Centre and Design Gallery, Leeds, p12; Dean Clough Contemporary Art Gallery, Halifax, p43; Doncaster MBC: Cultural Services Division, p64; Eastthorpe Gallery, Mirfield, p49; Green Man Gallery, Pickering, p73; Henry Moore Sculpture Trust Studio, Halifax, p44 (photo: Werner J Hannappel); Godfrey and Twatt, Harrogate, p25; Gordon Reece Gallery, Knaresborough, p27; Harrogate Museum and Art Gallery Services, p23, 24, 26; Hull City Council: Museums & Art Galleries, p81, 82; Jewell & Roberts, Holmfirth, p50; Kirklees Metropolitan Council: Cultural Services, p52; Kirklees Leisure Services: Libraries & Arts, p41; King's Manor Gallery, York, p31; Leeds Art Space Society, p14; Leeds City Art Galleries, frontispiece (photo: John Freeman), p11 (photo: Leeds City Council Planning Dept); Linton Court Gallery, Settle, p35; Look Gallery, Helmsley, p38; Metropolitan Borough of Rotherham, p65; Middlesbrough Borough Council: Leisure Services Dept, p79; National Museum of Photography, Film & TV, p8; Sheffield City Art Galleries, p59, 60, 67; Sutcliffe Gallery, Whitby, p71; Throstle Nest Gallery, Huddersfield, p48; Untitled Gallery, Sheffield, p68; Wakefield Art Galleries and Museums, p56; Yorkshire Sculpture Park, p54, 55 (photos: Jerry Hardman Jones).

The map on page xi was drawn by David Leather.

INTRODUCTION

This guide is intended for all those people for whom a pleasant day out, a visit or a holiday will, if they are lucky, include a memorable encounter with a good gallery in an unexpected place or a browse through an interesting collection in a major town. I hope it will take the element of luck out of such encounters and help in the planning stages of any trip to or in Yorkshire.

Yorkshire residents who think they know their county and its attractions will discover reasons to revisit places they know well and search out some far-flung corners. Holiday-makers and visitors passing through may want to make a detour or extend a stopover to include a few hours picture gazing. Other places of interest to art lovers with time to spare are also mentioned.

I hope this book will also serve to celebrate the richness of our provincial public galleries, which contain many little-known gems and nationally important individual items and collections.

In making my selection of private galleries, I have had to employ a personal yardstick which may cause dissent. There are many outlets which call themselves galleries which I term picture or art gift shops, which, while catering admirably for a particular market, do not add significantly to the contemporary art scene by their choice of exhibitors. Craft galleries showing the work of good regional potters, weavers, jewellers and others are, however, listed.

Given the size of the county, I know I may have missed a gallery worthy of inclusion or a recent addition to the scene, and I hope that readers who discover a delight unknown to me will pass on their secret, via the publishers, so that a possible reprinting can be updated. In these uncertain economic times it may also happen that a gallery has closed before you get there and the same information would be welcome. Since some changes are always inevitable between research and publication, and subsequently, a phone call to check before a visit is wise.

I would like to thank Pat Laycock who has assisted me with the research for this book – which has involved many miles and hours of looking – and also those galleries and individuals who responded to requests for help, information and illustrations. A useful book which gave me added insights into the history of our public galleries is *Treasures For The People* by P Brears and S Davies, published by Yorkshire and Humberside Museums Council in 1989. My thanks, too, to Smith Settle for seeing the need for such a guide, which I hope will become a well-thumbed addition to glove compartments, pockets and handbags.

Mary Sara
1992

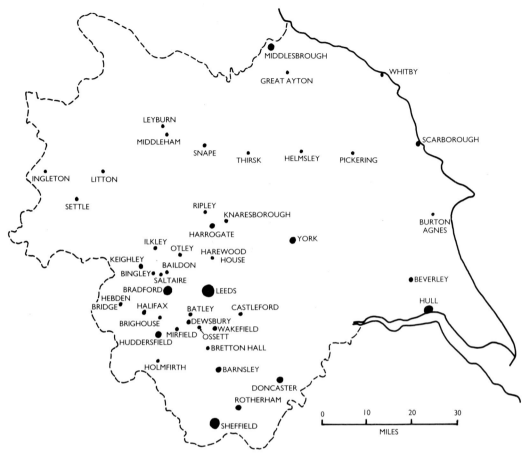

MIDDLESBROUGH

GREAT AYTON

WHITBY

SCARBOROUGH

LEYBURN

MIDDLEHAM

SNAPE

THIRSK

HELMSLEY

PICKERING

INGLETON

LITTON

SETTLE

RIPLEY

KNARESBOROUGH

BURTON AGNES

HARROGATE

YORK

ILKLEY

OTLEY

HAREWOOD HOUSE

KEIGHLEY

BAILDON

BINGLEY

SALTAIRE

BEVERLEY

BRADFORD

LEEDS

HEBDEN BRIDGE

HALIFAX

BATLEY

CASTLEFORD

HULL

BRIGHOUSE

DEWSBURY

WAKEFIELD

MIRFIELD

OSSETT

HUDDERSFIELD

BRETTON HALL

HOLMFIRTH

BARNSLEY

DONCASTER

ROTHERHAM

SHEFFIELD

0   10   20   30

MILES

Map Showing the Location of the Galleries

LEEDS AND BRADFORD

The image of smoke-filled valleys punctuated by hundreds of tall chimneys, blackened mills and tiers of terraced houses encamped around them as far as the eye can see, pervades the public consciousness when the West Riding woollen towns are mentioned. Such a picture may come from early engravings reproduced in school history books on the Industrial Revolution, when the burgeoning civic pride of nineteenth century mill owners and merchants delighted in such evidence of prosperity and progress. The more chimneys smoking, the more money was being made – or 'Where there's muck there's brass'. Alongside their investment in mills, inventions of new machinery and thus greater returns for themselves, many developed a taste for the arts. Self-improvement and the display of wealth or culture may have been their initial motivation, but once their own drawing rooms were suitably embellished with original works, they turned their energies to sharing their discernment with their fellow citizens.

They had a desire to see their town or city graced with imposing public buildings and visible signs of culture, and in this there was a strong element of competition between the various new boroughs. The provision of education and moral enlightenment through art for the masses, which took up Ruskin's ideas and reflected the strong nonconformist beliefs pertaining in the region, took many forms at the time. From mechanics institutes to museums and galleries, public parks to free concerts, these self-made men laid the foundations for much of what can still be seen and enjoyed by the citizenry of today. What began from pride and paternalism has survived and flowered into civic architecture of note and fine collections of art. With historical hindsight, we might wish they had given as much thought, energy and money to the conditions of the workers whose labour they prospered from, because some of the effects of that legacy, too, can still be seen in the tightly-packed airless streets, polluted rivers and blackened stones. It can also be seen, ironically, in the many industrial museums in the area, which, whilst celebrating and recording the machines, also illustrate the misery of their operatives.

The fast-flowing becks and rivers, which provided the power for the early mechanisation of the previously cottage-based spinning and weaving industry, still divide and sculpt the landscape. Their green valleys also provided the refuge for the urban middle classes, who, with the coming of the railways, built their villas and brought culture to previously rural hamlets such as Ilkley. The River Aire which flows through Leeds flows first through Keighley, and the building of the Leeds-Liverpool Canal beside its course ensured the continuing industrialisation of that valley. The Wharfe Valley in which Ilkley lies was not so despoiled.

Today, the visitor who looks down over Bradford from the surrounding hills, or who drives through Leeds, sees few chimneys. Even in the last ten years, many have disappeared. The air is clean and the rivers are recovering, while the countless streets of terraces and

Portrait of Samuel Cunliffe Lister by John Collier. Lister was typical of the philanthropic Victorian businessmen who founded many of today's galleries and museums.

back-to-back houses are re-pointed or sand-blasted, paved and leafy. Sadly, much of the best Victorian public architecture was lost in the mania for modernism which swept through many Northern cities in the postwar years, but enough remains for the imagination to work upon. Some of the grandest survivors are the great stone Bradford mills themselves and the redbrick wharf-side warehouses of Leeds. The textile trade slumped in the twentieth century, but some specialist producers managed to rise above the flood of imports and adverse trading conditions. Some mills found new uses and new life, others were demolished and are remembered now only in street names.

An artistic voyager to Leeds and Bradford will find plenty to admire and enjoy in the industrial heritage still visible by the canalside and in the valley bottoms, but cannot leave without a sense of the rich variety of visual arts – both past and present – available to local and visitor alike. The immigration of a variety of ethnic groups from Europe and Asia means that both cities have a lively multicultural flavour. This is no new phenomenon, however; for instance, Leeds was host and protector to many Jewish immigrants over the last century, and Bradford has its Little Germany area. Present day awareness means that all strands of the current population's origins are properly respected and represented in exhibition programmes and collections. Both cities have their universities and art schools, which have produced many outstanding and famous artists of international reputation. The extent of public participation in the arts through visiting galleries and education and outreach programmes is difficult to quantify, but the impression remains that it is unusually high in Yorkshire in comparison to the rest of the country. Indeed, the richness and quality of the arts draws many visitors, and councils are aware of its economic significance to the area.

CARTWRIGHT HALL, LISTER PARK, MANNINGHAM LANE, BRADFORD. Tel: (0274) 493313. Daily 10-6 (5pm from 1st Oct), closed Mondays (except Bank Holidays). Cafe. Toilets. Request assistance for disabled – lift and wheelchair available.

BRADFORD CITY ART GALLERY at Cartwright Hall in Lister Park (to the north-west of the city centre on the A650 towards Keighley) grew out of and reflects the area's commercial foundation on wool and steam power. Named after Edmund Cartwright, whose invention of a wool-combing machine created the wealth that enabled Samuel Lister to give both Lister Park and the gallery to his city, Cartwright Hall opened in 1904. A ninety-three year old ex-Bradfordian remembers the spectacular exhibition that covered the park to celebrate the opening – with curiosities such as an African village and her first encounter as a five year old with black skins and faces.

Cartwright Hall, Bradford.

The hall's grandiose baroque bulk sits among neat flowerbeds in what was once the favoured residential district of Bradford's wool merchants and industrialists. Their prosperous Victorian mansions are now less well favoured, though still stand among leafy streets overlooking the park.

At the heart of the building, on entering, is the sculpture court, a light-filled well from which stone stairs lead to the upper galleries. Four ground floor galleries are used for a constantly changing high-quality exhibition programme. Many are originated by Cartwright staff, and reflect the rich and fascinating multicultural nature of the present Bradford

The sculpture court in Cartwright Hall.

population, as well as providing opportunities to celebrate the wealth of artistic talent of the region. Weekend workshops and its popularity with families who stroll in the park, wander the exhibitions and linger with ice creams from the small cafe, mean that the Cartwright is a well-used leisure facility. The acclaimed and very popular British International Print Biennale takes place here and it extends into much of the available space, including the large upstairs gallery.

It is on this level, among panelled walls and polished floors, that the visitor can view part of the extensive permanent collection. The Victorian predilection for classical subjects and barely suppressed erotica is reflected in such works as Edwin Long's huge *An Egyptian Feast* and Wright Barker's bare-breasted *Circe*, who greets Odysseus among tame lions and strewn poppy heads. The Edwardians are well represented, with fine examples by Henry La Thangue and Sir George Clausen, and the English Impressionists by Buxton Knight, Fred Stead and Stanhope Forbes among others. There is usually a selection from their holdings of Pre-Raphaelite drawings on display, and the often reproduced *The Brown Boy* by Sir Joshua Reynolds (now thought to be largely by his assistants) can be seen. It is to be hoped on your visit that some of Bradford's many fine David Hockney prints, drawings and paintings given by the artist and his family will be on view, or that a thematic exhibition drawn from the collection will demonstrate the depth and interest contained in the basement stores of art, which represent every facet of twentieth century developments. Examples of the highly-glazed and colourful Burmantofts pottery punctuate the Victorian and Edwardian rooms.

In this area of Bradford are some of the best Asian restaurants, and not far away, commanding the skyline, is Samuel Lister's magnificent mill, famous for the production of velvets and soon to house part of the Victoria and Albert Museum's collection.

Arguably Bradford's most famous artistic son, David Hockney, has the **1853 GALLERY**, Saltaire, all to himself thanks to the philanthropic, entrepreneurial spirit of local businessman Jonathan Silver. Taking the Keighley road from Cartwright Hall brings you to Saltaire, the attractively-conserved model village and mill built by Sir Titus Salt for his workers in 1853. 10,000 square feet of the spinning shed, with its arched windows, redbrick vaulted ceiling and cast-iron pillars, forms the showcase for Mr Silver's personal collection of Hockneys. The scale of the space, the architectural quality of the surrounding buildings and the highly idiosyncratic nature of the display makes a visit an unusual gallery-going experience. The Commonwealth Institute's new Northern Regional Centre now occupies part of the mill complex and includes a small gallery.

1853 GALLERY, VICTORIA ROAD, SALTAIRE. Tel: (0274) 531163. Daily 10-5. Full disabled access. Shop. Toilets. Cafe nearby.

The 1853 Gallery, Saltaire, with its owner Jonathan Silver.

INDUSTRIAL MUSEUM, MOORSIDE ROAD, BRADFORD. Tel: (0274) 631756. Daily 10-5, closed Mondays (except Bank Holidays). Cafe. Shop. Limited access for disabled.

Approximately three miles from the centre of Bradford just off the A658 Harrogate Road is the **BRADFORD INDUSTRIAL MUSEUM**, housed in the converted Moorside Mills — a typical range of mill buildings once used for worsted spinning. As well as offering a fascinating and comprehensive overview of the district's industrial heritage, which includes working machinery and engines, trams, Jowett cars (once produced in Bradford) and interpretive material, a space has been retained for exhibitions of art and crafts. There is usually a connection, however tenuous, with the nature of the museum — such as textiles or local history. Working horses, good parking, a cafe and some interesting buildings, including back-to-back houses, add to the pleasure of a visit.

NATIONAL MUSEUM OF PHOTOGRAPHY, FILM AND TELEVISION, PRINCES VIEW, BRADFORD. Tel: (0274) 727488. Tuesday-Sunday 10-6. Cafe. Shop. Lifts to all floors and chair lift on stairs. Good access for disabled.

In the very heart of the city, between the library and Alhambra Theatre, it is impossible to miss the **NATIONAL MUSEUM OF PHOTOGRAPHY, FILM AND TELE-VISION**. The remarkable growth and development of this museum since it opened in 1983 has been part of Bradford's successful attempt to put the city on the national tourist and cultural map, and it won the Museum of the Year Award in

The National Museum of Photography.

1988. It is a bustling 'hands-on' type of experience, with many interactive displays as well as static exhibits and exhibitions. A single day would seem hardly long enough were you to attempt to thoroughly absorb all the information on offer, but breaks for snacks in the restaurant overlooking the city centre or to take in a film on the amazing Imax screen, Europe's largest, offer respite. The art of photography is not forgotten among the history of technical developments and examples of modern techno-logical wizardry. Exhibitions of the work of famous photo-graphers from Britain and the rest of the world, on all subjects from photo-journalism to portraits, thematic ex-hibitions and archive material, give quieter, more reflective moments for those interested in the art rather than the science of photography.

Another award winner is the **COLOUR MUSEUM**, which is only a few minutes walk from the Photographic Museum and was declared the Best Museum of Industrial or Social History by National Heritage in 1988. Founded and run by the Society of Dyers and Colourists, it has excellent

THE COLOUR MUSEUM, 82 GRATTAN ROAD, BRADFORD. Tel: (0274) 390955. Tuesday-Friday 2-5, Saturday 10-4. Shop. Limited access for disabled. Admission charge

Treadwell's Art Mill, Bradford.

visitor-operated displays which deliver educative material entertainingly. Art lovers may find that the displays on textile printing and explorations of concepts of colour make a detour worthwhile.

In the historic Little Germany area of Bradford, on the hill behind the cathedral, 32,000 square feet of former wool mill constitutes the venue for **TREADWELL'S ART MILL** – a private commercial venture. Entry is via that rarity, a good vegetarian cafe, and above are four vast floors of what can best be termed as humanist/realist art. Paintings and sculpture in a realist style, often dealing with the less

TREADWELL'S ART MILL, UPPER PARK GATE, LITTLE GERMANY, BRADFORD. Tel: (0274) 306065. Daily 10-6. Entrance charge, children under 5 free, concessions. Vegetarian cafe. Shop.

attractive aspects of human behaviour but sprinkled with humour and laced with skills and insight, provide an experience to make you think and blink when you emerge, dazed, hours later.

Bradford lacks a really high-quality contemporary private gallery, but the **HAZELROYD GALLERY**, just down the hill from Treadwell's, features work by some of the region's popular landscape artists.

Three miles west of the city centre on the B6145 is Thornton village, the birthplace of the Brontës, which has a small artistic community at **SOUTH SQUARE**. Studios and workshops, cafe and gallery provide an outlet and showcase for local and regional artists and craftspeople, and their work.

Whilst in Bradford, Bolling Hall, a mile from the city centre off the A650 Wakefield road, is worth a visit. Built and extended from medieval times to the eighteenth century, the house now exists cheek-by-jowl with urban housing estates, but it has a very welcoming and restful atmosphere, and good period furnishings and furniture.

In Leeds, next to Cuthbert Brodrick's imposing town hall stands the **CITY ART GALLERY**. Five minutes' walk from the station and close to the commercial and shopping centres, it makes a good central starting point for a visit to Leeds. In a small gallery next to the restaurant is a watercolour of the town hall in 1854, a lithograph of J Atkinson Grimshaw's *Boar Lane By Lamplight* and a pen and wash view of redbrick terraces by a local contemporary artist. This identification with the history and culture of the city is only one aspect of a gallery whose central position among the thronging shoppers and office workers identifies its activities with its wide audience. Like Cartwright Hall, it has its foundations in local patronage which, spurred by the jubilee celebrations of 1887, resulted in its opening in 1888. The original building has been much extended since then, most obviously by the front portion which is home to the Henry Moore Sculpture Gallery. The permanent collection has both breadth and depth, and major touring and Leeds-originated exhibitions make up an annual programme which

HAZELROYD GALLERY, MERCHANT'S HOUSE, 25 PECKOVER STREET, LITTLE GERMANY, BRADFORD. Tel: (0274) 309715. Monday-Friday 9.30-4, Saturday 10-2, but phone to check.

SOUTH SQUARE COMMUNITY ARTS WORKSHOPS AND GALLERY, 377 THORNTON ROAD, THORNTON, BRADFORD. Tel: (0274) 834747. Tuesday-Saturday 11-5, Sunday 1-4.30.

LEEDS CITY ART GALLERY, THE HEADROW, LEEDS. Tel: (0532) 478248. Monday-Friday 10-6, Wednesday 10-9, Saturday 10-4, Sunday 2-5. 90% disabled access, disabled toilets. Restaurant. Library.

Leeds City Art Gallery.

is always interesting. Workshops, lectures, library, print loan scheme and a popular cafe mean that the gallery is well used by Leeds people.

The visitor new to the North will perhaps be surprised how many well-known pictures they have seen frequently reproduced actually belong to the Leeds Collection. Tissot's *The Bridesmaid, The Return of Persephone* by Lord Leighton, Lady Butler's *Scotland For Ever*, Wyndham Lewis's *Praxitella* and *Christ's Entry Into Jerusalem* by Stanley Spencer are just a few of the more obviously familiar items. The Leeds holdings of English watercolours are very fine, but the collection is as eclectic as one could hope for. Each visitor will find their own favourite area of enquiry rewarded. Most of the notable artists of the last 150 years of art are

The Craft and Design Gallery, part of Leeds City Art Gallery.

represented, from Picasso to Keith Vaughan, Manet to Jacob Kramer (an adopted Leeds artist), William Etty to Andy Goldsworthy, some lovely small Corots, Whistler and Wadsworth – the list is long. The greater spaciousness of the building allows a larger part of the permanent collection to be on show than at Bradford, and the display of twentieth century British art, particularly the British Surrealists (for instance Tristram Hillier and Roland Penrose), is very informative and well displayed.

Many fine twentieth century artists have been connected with Leeds, the most important being Henry Moore. The specially-created sculpture galleries provide space for the permanent display of works by him and other noted recent and contemporary sculptors, and on occasion for exhibitions by leading contemporary practitioners.

CRAFT CENTRE AND DESIGN GALLERY, CITY ART GALLERY, THE HEADROW, LEEDS. Tel: (0532) 478241. Tuesday-Saturday 10-5.30, Thursday 10-7pm. Full disabled access.

Below the sculpture galleries is the **LEEDS CRAFT AND DESIGN GALLERY**. Although limited for space, a very wide range of contemporary crafts is shown, all of the highest standard. Ceramics, jewellery, furniture, textiles and glass chosen from around the country – but also featuring the work of regional craftspeople – are sensitively displayed. Solo shows by potters have introduced some of the most exciting and beautiful ceramics being produced today to a Northern audience, and the Christmas craft jewellery show justifiably draws the crowds. From time to time, prints and smaller pictures are also exhibited.

LEEDS UNIVERSITY GALLERY, PARKINSON BUILDING, WOODHOUSE LANE, LEEDS. Tel: (0532) 332777. Open term time only, Monday-Friday 10-5. Disabled access and toilets.

During university term times, the **LEEDS UNIVER-SITY GALLERY** runs a stimulating exhibition programme. Alongside the permanent display from the Irene Manton Bequest, visitors may find a thematic selection from the university's excellent collection, a good regional painter or artists from any number of disciplines. Whatever the nature of the shows, one of the great pleasures of a visit is the excellence of the hanging. The university is signed from the city centre on the A660 and the gallery is in the unmistakable white-towered Parkinson Building next to the main road.

LEEDS POLYTECHNIC GALLERY, CALVERLEY STREET, LEEDS. Tel: (0532) 832600. Monday-Friday 10-5, Saturday 10-3. Disabled access and toilets.

Whilst in that area, a short walk back down the hill will bring you to the **LEEDS POLYTECHNIC GALLERY**, also fronting on to the road. The architecture of this complex is not liked by locals, and stories of lost souls trying to get out and, having done so, never returning may be more than apocryphal. The gallery space – whilst easy to access – is awkward to manage from a curatorial point of view, being a cube dissected by stairs and a half floor. Shows there tend to reflect the experimental, conceptual and ideological developments of the moment, in all media.

An installation The Room *by Louis Wilde at Leeds Art Space Society.*

Next to the West Yorkshire Playhouse, which is signed from most junctions in the city, the **YORKSHIRE DANCE CENTRE** has a foyer exhibition space where dance-related art is shown. Walk beyond the West Yorkshire Playhouse (which has what it calls the **NEWLYN GALLERY** but which is simply a wall near the entrance to the Courtyard Theatre), under the railway bridge and then look for a brick warehouse to your left above Maris Street Motors. This is home to the **LEEDS ART SPACE SOCIETY**. The studio space movement which has grown up in the last few years provides, through self-help, cheap spaces and a supportive environment for young and less established artists. Two huge floors have been partitioned into cubicles and spaces, the decay and dirt being masked and defeated by liberal quantities of paint and enthusiasm.

YORKSHIRE DANCE CENTRE, 3 ST PETERS BUILDINGS, ST PETERS SQUARE, LEEDS. Tel: (0532) 426066. Open 9-9 weekdays, 10 – 4 weekends.

NEWLYN GALLERY, WEST YORKSHIRE PLAYHOUSE, QUARRY HILL MOUNT, LEEDS. Tel: (0532) 442111. Monday-Saturday 10am-11pm. Restaurant, cafe, bars. Shop. Disabled access and toilets.

WORKSPACE, LEEDS ART SPACE SOCIETY, MARIS STREET, off MILL STREET, LEEDS. Tel: (0532) 434252. Phone for opening hours.

The members have also created an exhibition area called Workspace, and invite artists to make site-specific works or installations. It is a place to see interesting work in many styles, to pick out a future winner in the art stakes, to admire the tenacity of people who must be artists, and enjoy a range of media and manners of expression.

Here you are close to the River Aire, and recently rescued and redeveloped areas of handsome wharf and warehouse architecture. At 46 The Calls is the **DESIGN INNOVATION CENTRE**, which runs a varied programme of exhibitions in the reception area. Walking back towards the centre and markets area, Leeds's mercantile and industrial past is enshrined in such buildings as Cuthbert Brodrick's elliptical Corn Exchange and the eighteenth century White Cloth Hall. Pause for a moment on the steps outside the Corn Exchange, look to your right and a twentieth century addition to the civic art of Leeds can be seen above the bus shelters. Local painter Graeme Willson has produced an allegorical mural incorporating mythological associations with fertility, the corn goddess and architectural references. The same artist is responsible for an earlier mural on a theme of inner city renewal, which overlooks the Cookridge Street car park near the civic hall.

Just past the university going out of the city is a small octagonal building in the park called the **PAVILION**. This space is used to promote and encourage women photographers and visual artists, with a particular emphasis on Black women's art, through workshops, courses and exhibitions. Further out again, just past the Arndale Centre in Headingley, is Alma Road where the **BRAHM** advertising agency hold exhibitions of regional artists' work within their company headquarters.

Two other jewels in Leeds's crown which require short but extremely worthwhile journeys are Temple Newsam and Lotherton Hall. To stand in the vast courtyard of Temple Newsam (five miles east of the city off the A63 Leeds to Selby road) is to dive back in time to join the Elizabethan and Jacobean families who built it. The house is full of treasures of painting, furniture and silver, and much

DESIGN INNOVATION CENTRE, 46 THE CALLS, LEEDS. Tel: (0532) 458182. Monday-Friday 9-5.15. Disabled access and toilet.

THE PAVILION, WOODHOUSE MOOR, 235 WOODHOUSE LANE, LEEDS. Tel: (0532) 431749. Monday-Thursday 10-4. Disabled access and toilets.

BRAHM GALLERY, THE BRAHM BUILDING, 9A ALMA ROAD, HEADINGLEY, LEEDS. Tel: (0532) 304000. Monday-Friday 9.30-5.30. Disabled access and toilets.

scholarly effort is still in progress to continue the process of restoration and conservation. Twelve miles north-east of the city, just off the A1 at Aberford, Lotherton Hall is a younger but equally fascinating building. Furnishings reflect its heyday as an Edwardian country house, but there are also displays of costume, porcelain, paintings and pottery – including a good selection of twentieth century works.

North of Leeds, Harewood House is a honeypot for tourists, but the art lover will find the **TERRACE GALLERY** an additional incentive for a visit. Cool, stone-flagged rooms under the terrace have been skilfully converted to provide a pleasing venue for a very wide range of exhibitions.

THE TERRACE GALLERY, HAREWOOD HOUSE, LEEDS. Tel: (0532) 886225. Daily 11-4.30. Shop. Restaurant. Access difficult.

When Victorian Bradford wool merchants tired of the increasingly polluted suburbs of their city, they looked northwards to the soft green valley of the Wharfe to build their villas. Here a small spa town was already expanding due to the advent of the railway. Ilkley had been invaded by settlers before – the Romans established a fort on a mound overlooking the river but abandoned the site in the late fourth and early fifth century AD. The site was subsequently the focus for medieval settlement, and parts of the largely late sixteenth century building known as the **MANOR HOUSE** can be identified as fourteenth century. Set in a quiet stone-paved square, entered through an archway from the busy A65 Leeds to Skipton road next to the parish church, it is an oasis of calm and pleasure.

THE MANOR HOUSE, CASTLE YARD, ILKLEY. Tel: (0943) 600066. Daily 10-6 (5pm from October 1st), closed Mondays (except Bank Holidays). Ground floor access to museum only for disabled. Toilets.

The house body is furnished in the style of a nineteenth century farmhouse, and, leading off it, a small museum succinctly records Ilkley's history from the prehistoric and Bronze Age people who left their curious carvings on the moor, through to the heyday of Ilkley as a Victorian spa. Upstairs is possibly one of the most attractive gallery spaces any small town could possess. Light streams through mullioned windows revealing polished wood floors, white walls and a magnificent 'king-post' trussed roof structure. An offshoot of Bradford City Art Galleries, it nevertheless has an exhibition programme with a distinctive flavour. It features contemporary art and crafts, frequently by artists

The Manor House, Ilkley.

from Yorkshire or with regional connections. The two connecting rooms are admirably suited to two person shows, and staff cope with uneven walls, sloping floors and the personality of the building itself with great ingenuity when hanging and displaying works.

A mile out of Ilkley in the adjoining suburb of Ben Rhydding, the **LAURON GALLERY** offers the kind of art which is very accessible and popular. Some of the artists stocked by the gallery (almost entirely landscapes) show empathy with their subjects and good observational and

LAURON GALLERY, 122 BOLLING ROAD, BEN RHYDDING, ILKLEY. Tel: (0943) 600725. Monday-Friday 9-1 and 2-6, Saturdays 9-5. Ground floor access.

drawing skills as well as facility with technique. The same criteria apply to the **GLENRHYDDING GALLERY** in Bondgate, Otley.

It is possible to approach Ilkley from Bradford over the moors via Baildon. This route gives the most breathtaking first view of the town and its valley as you round the Cow and Calf rocks, and also takes you past **BAILDON CRAFT WORKSHOPS** as you leave the A6038 via the B6151 between Shipley and Baildon. Fourteen small businesses, making a wide range of crafts from stained glass to wooden toys via soft furnishings and kites, are situated on the five floors of a converted chapel.

Three miles north-west of Ilkley, on the A65 to Skipton in the village of Addingham (on Bolton Road – turn right at the Crown), is a converted co-op warehouse. Here Eric and Meira Stockl live and work. Their **HELYG POTTERY** sells Eric's sturdy and sensitively-glazed and decorated domestic ware. Everything from a mug or small plate to a huge round-bellied casserole or set of goblets carries the unmistakable mark of a confident craftsman and fertile artist. Above, Meira weaves tapestries and rugs to commission and for exhibition. She works in a variety of ways – small personal pieces, lengths of Ikat silk and glowing rugs in subtle strong colours, and also sells well-chosen ethnic and tribal textiles from India and other parts of Asia. From time to time, exhibitions include the work of other artists and potters from the locality.

The journey from the Wharfe Valley over to the Aire is instructive. The former became the dormitory for Leeds and Bradford's middle classes and remained little touched by industry, but the Aire Valley town of Keighley throbbed to the turning of mills and engines from the days of the last handloom weavers to the textile recession of the 1960s. On the outskirts of the town, off the A629 Skipton Road, lies **CLIFFE CASTLE**, a pile of baronial proportions. Eclectic in style, it has been described as 'probably the last of the Victorian fantasies'. The exterior is less fancifully embellished now than when local textile magnate Henry Isaac Butterfield completed his castle in the 1880s, but some of

GLENRHYDDING GALLERY, 38 BONDGATE, OTLEY. Tel: (0943) 466323. Monday-Saturday 10-5, Sunday 2-5. Partial access for disabled.

BAILDON CRAFT WORKSHOPS, BROWGATE, BAILDON. Tel: (0274) 594946. Tuesday-Sunday 10-5. Toilet. No disabled access.

HELYG POTTERY, BOLTON ROAD, ADDINGHAM, ILKLEY. Tel: (0943) 830165. Weekdays 9-5. Phone for other times.

CLIFFE CASTLE, SPRING GARDENS LANE, KEIGHLEY. Tel: (0535) 758230. Daily 10-6 (5pm from October 1st), closed Mondays (except Bank Holidays). Limited disabled access. Toilet. Cafe in park.

WHAT IS A ROCK?

*'Molecules to Minerals' at Cliffe Castle,
Keighley.*

the reception rooms have been painstakingly recreated with either original or period furniture and furnishings. His tastes included French Empire and Gothic, and he lavished a fortune on imported objects, pictures and furniture – all displayed in cluttered, over-dressed Victorian style.

The ballroom houses a comprehensive natural history museum, and there are also excellent displays on the geological history of the Aire Valley, minerals and local history. Where the kitchens, larders and pantries once stood, a large octagonal hall was created in the 1950s after the conversion of the house to a museum. Here temporary exhibitions fill the floor, walls and balconied walls above.

Although they are often related directly to the nature of the collections or local history and industry, touring shows on a variety of themes also visit.

East Riddlesden Hall, a mile from Keighley on the road to Bingley and Bradford, is a lovely seventeenth century merchant's house owned by the National Trust. Its Great Barn is worth a detour, as is the tranquil setting, surprising among the industry, roads and houses.

About a mile and a half along the A650 towards Bradford from East Riddlesden is the turning left to Micklethwaite, a delightful hilly village where the **STUDIO WORKSHOPS** at Holroyd Mill are worth searching out, although dificult to find and having steep access. Once the building was an early nineteenth century water-powered mill, now it provides studio workshops and display gallery for a furniture maker and carpenter, potter and painter.

MICKLETHWAITE STUDIO WORKSHOPS, HOLROYD MILL, BECK ROAD, MICKLETHWAITE, nr BINGLEY. Tel: (0274) 561209. Daily 10-4, except Christmas Day/Boxing Day.

If decorative bric-à-brac, interior decoration, hand-painted furniture and similar nostalgia for the past interest you, it might be worth finding the mill gallery of **DESIGNS ON YOU** in Dalton Lane not far from Keighley Station.

DESIGNS ON YOU, DALTON MILLS, DALTON LANE, KEIGHLEY. Tel: (0535) 608028. Monday-Friday 10.30-5.30, Saturday and Sunday 11-5. Shop. No disabled access.

When in Keighley it is impossible to forget that we are in 'Brontë Country', and a trip to Haworth would seem inevitable. Choose a winter weekday if you wish to enjoy the delights of the village and the atmosphere of the parsonage to the full. Haworth is full of shops selling pictures and prints, but none which, in the context of this guide, I would recommend as a gallery to search for.

HARROGATE AND YORK

The spa town of Harrogate lives up to its image of manicured gardens, delectable Georgian and Victorian architecture, elegant shops and more antique boutiques per square mile than anywhere else in the country. The polite conservatism of such a place, despite its bustling conference trade, can be stifling and it is possible, briefly, to forget that other modes of less well-heeled living exist. An observant and humorous eye for people-watching, as well as the visual pleasure bestowed by order, conservation and history, can add a grace note of wit to a visit. Untouched by the Industrial Revolution, Harrogate's present status and character are founded on the sulphurous waters believed to be so beneficial to the health of Georgian and Victorian England. The Pump Room, baths, grand hotels, leafy gardens and excellent shops which catered for gouty gentlemen and vaporous ladies now serve a rich hinterland of landed money, commuting professionals and the modern tourist market alike.

Knaresborough, three miles to the east of Harrogate on the road to York, lies in a gorge cut by the River Nidd. A lovely parish church, castle ruins and the river itself offer visual delights, as do the tumbling houses, narrow streets and lively market. It is famous for its petrifying Dropping Well and Mother Shipton's prophecies, and lies in the rich undulating farmland of Nidderdale.

The problem facing any visitor to York, whatever their particular interest, is – where to start? To ensure that your day begins well, leave your car at home, park and ride or go by train if possible. It is a compact city and one best discovered on foot. The loveliness and fame of the Minster brings millions to its streets throughout the year, but everywhere one walks and looks the history books come to life. A centre for trade, political power, education, culture and religion for a thousand years or more, the evidence of how such a place attracted excellence in artists, craftsmen and builders is on hand throughout the city. In museums and archeological digs, in the Minster's undercroft, above eye level in the Shambles or any of the medieval streets, and above all walking on and looking down from the city walls, history jogs the mind constantly.

The late twentieth century likes to package experience in visitor centres, theme parks and reconstructions of the past, but the sensitive visitor to York has no need of such aids to the imagination. The ghosts of Roman soldiers, Viking traders and medieval monks rub shoulders with yeoman farmers, eighteenth century scholars and nineteenth century railway magnates. The lovely Vale of York, with its comfortable farms, country estates and lazily looping rivers, provided the wealth on which the mercantile city prospered, and on which the comparatively recent cultural attributes of galleries and museums flourished.

If old masters (note the lower case) are your taste in art, then the many antique establishments in Harrogate offer an abundance of choice. Galleries attempting to show and sell good contemporary art beyond the bland and popular landscape tradition have, sadly, rarely lasted long in Harrogate. Inhabitants with modern tastes have largely had to buy elsewhere.

In times of recession, perhaps only Harrogate could have found the energy and means to open new premises for its public art collection – the **MERCER ART GALLERY**. Built in 1805, the Promenade Room – where takers of the waters in the adjacent Royal Pump Room were wont to perambulate – is a lovely building to visit, and the restoration and adaptation has been sensitively done. The collection from which displays are selected is fairly typical of its kind, but has enough good and interesting items to hold the attention. Like many such provincial art galleries, it had its genesis as an adjunct to the public library. On my first visit after it opened in April 1991, I noted such varied delights as a witty Joseph Crawhall, two very nice Christopher Woods and a pair of equally fine Atkinson Grimshaws – one the lovely *Silver Moonlight*. Twentieth century British art is well represented, with works by (among others) Sickert, Lessore, Paul Nash, David Bomberg and Wyndham Lewis. In addition, naive paintings by Joseph Baker Fountain and antiquarian items from the eclectic Kent Collection will be joined from time to time by temporary exhibitions.

Unlike contemporary art, contemporary crafts have a good showcase and selling venue in Harrogate in the form of a small shop upstairs in the Westminster Arcade off

THE MERCER GALLERY, SWAN ROAD, HARROGATE. Tel: (0423) 503340. Tuesday-Saturday 10-5, Sunday 2-5, closed Monday. Disabled access.

Opposite: Ratisbon Cathedral by Samuel Prout (1783-1852) in the Harrogate Collection.

The Mercer Art Gallery, Harrogate.

Parliament Street. Since 1985, **GODFREY AND TWATT** have been showing ceramics, jewellery, glass, carvings and original prints from leading British makers, including many from Yorkshire. Standards are high, the range adventurous, and as well as constantly changing stock, individual makers are featured four or five times a year.

GODFREY AND TWATT, 7 WESTMINSTER ARCADE, PARLIAMENT STREET, HARROGATE. Tel: (0423) 525300. Monday-Saturday 10-5.30. No disabled access.

Just north of Harrogate, Ripley is a pleasant pottering place with its castle, church and tidily picturesque estate village. The **CHANTRY HOUSE GALLERY** in the village centre stocks pleasant though largely undemanding paintings in various media, and prints by Yorkshire artists.

THE CHANTRY HOUSE GALLERY, MAIN STREET, RIPLEY. Tel: (0423) 770141. Open daily 10-5 except Monday and Friday, Sunday 2-5. Disabled access.

The **GORDON REECE GALLERY** in Knaresborough, on the left up the hill from the station, is nationally renowned for its selling exhibitions of rugs, killims, and other textiles and fascinating artefacts from all over the Middle and Far East. It seems strange to discover such exotica in a small Yorkshire market town – like finding a bird of paradise among the pigeons. Gordon Reece has

GORDON REECE GALLERY, FINKLE STREET, KNARESBOROUGH. Tel: (0423) 866219. Daily 10.30-5, closed Thursdays, Sunday 2-5, closed January and beginning of February.

24

An example of Godfrey and Twatt's ceramics: Two-Storey Teapot *by Dennis Farrell.*

GORDON REECE CERAMICS GALLERY, 8 KIRKGATE, KNARESBOROUGH. Tel: (0423) 866219. Hours as above.

recently opened another outlet in the town – **GORDON REECE CERAMICS** on Kirkgate off the market square. Here fine antique, oriental and non-European ceramics, and tribal and folk pottery are shown.

The Gordon Reece Gallery, Knaresborough.

YORK CITY ART GALLERY, EXHIBITION SQUARE, YORK. Tel: (0904) 623839. Monday-Saturday 10-5, Sunday 2.30-5. Good disabled access and toilets. Shop.

Left: First of the Ebb *(1938) by Edward Wadsworth, in the Harrogate Collection.*

In the appropriately-named Exhibition Square near Bootham Bar, **YORK CITY ART GALLERY** is a good place to begin for art lovers. A part of the present building was opened in 1879 for the purpose of holding a 'Yorkshire Fine Art and Industrial Exhibition', and the basis of its art collection came from a local bequest, as did so many contemporaneous collections throughout the country. It looks a rather severe and dour building from the outside, but contains riches within.

Whenever my visual palette is jaded from looking at too much that is mediocre or of questionable value, I find a visit to a major public collection refreshing. One is reminded of

27

standards of excellence from every era by which to judge today's art. As well as hosting important touring shows and locally-generated exhibitions, York's permanent collection has depth and breadth. Elizabethan portraits, an excellent selection of William Etty nudes, good seventeenth century Dutch works, the marvellous 1623 Domenichino fanatical-eyed *Portrait of Monsieur Aguech*, Fantin Latour roses, Lowry's *Peel Park* and Gwen John's *Girl In A Red Shawl* add up to a almost a surfeit of pleasure. Good examples by Gilman and Gore, and Paul Nash's seminal *Winter Sea*, are

Domenichino's Portrait of Monsieur Aguech *(1623) in York City Art Gallery.*

also memorable, though each visitor will find their own favourites in a collection which has few missing links. Lovers of twentieth century studio ceramics will enjoy the small but excellent Milner-White Collection which includes examples from the hands of Bernard Leach, Michael Cardew, Shoji Hamada and Katharine Pleydell-Bouverie.

KING'S MANOR GALLERY, EXHIBITION SQUARE, YORK. Tel: (0904) 433942. Daily 10-5, Sunday 2-5.

Immediately adjacent to the City Art Gallery is **KING'S MANOR**, a thirteenth century house which is part of the University of York. After wandering through its quiet courtyards – a pleasure in itself – go down the steps into a splendid converted cellar. A series of temporary shows – approximately two per university term – offer a wide experience of contemporary art via an eclectic programme which includes local practitioners.

THE STONEGATE GALLERY, 52A STONEGATE, YORK. Tel: (0904) 635141. Open April to October and Christmas, Tuesday-Saturday 10.30-5.

A five minute walk brings you to Stonegate, where through a little alleyway or snicket can be found the **STONEGATE GALLERY**. One-person shows succeed each other in this small space from April to October. Most of the exhibitors are from the region and the majority are landscape painters, though once a year local architects show their artistic skills and there is a mixed show at Christmas.

PYRAMID, 43 STONEGATE, YORK. Tel: (0904) 641187. Monday-Saturday 9.30-5.

Also on Stonegate is **PYRAMID** – a very good craft gallery selling high-quality crafts including glass, jewellery and pottery, mostly from Yorkshire craftspeople.

A riverside walk in York can encourage as much contemplation about the history of the city as any of its buildings, museums or interpretative centres. Crossing at Ouse Bridge near King's Staith brings one to Micklegate, which leads up to yet another of the city's 'bars' or gateways. The **BAR CONVENT MUSEUM AND GAL-**

THE BAR CONVENT MUSEUM, 17 BLOSSOM STREET, YORK. Tel: (0904) 643238. Tuesday-Saturday 10-4.30, open Bank Holidays, closed January. Cafe. Shop. Partial disabled access.

LERY can also be reached by dropping down from a walk around the city walls. The Georgian building by Thomas Atkinson provides the first attraction. A glazed courtyard with a curiously Moorish flavour is at the centre of the museum which is devoted to the history of Christianity in the North of England and the life of Mary Ward, foundress of the Institute of the Blessed Virgin Mary. There is a hidden neoclassical chapel – its dome invisible from outside the building since it is covered by a pitched roof – and in

Pyramid, on Stonegate, York.

adjoining rooms a gallery has been created which, by its varied programme of contemporary art and displays of historical or archeological interest, adds considerably to the richness of York's art scene.

Continuing away from the city along Blossom Street, past the Mount and turning left along Albemarle Road, brings you to Scarcroft Hill and the **KENTMERE HOUSE GALLERY**. In an Edwardian house overlooking York's famous

KENTMERE HOUSE GALLERY, 53 SCARCROFT HILL, YORK. Tel: (0904) 656507. Open every Thursday evening 6-9, and the first weekend of every month Saturday and Sunday 11-5. Other times, ring for an appointment.

King's Manor Gallery, York.

Knavesmire and racecourse, the owner shows the work of selected artists, both nationally known and relatively unknown, in the informal setting of her own home. Paintings and prints all show an eye for quality, and the service offered includes a library of illustrations and advice on framing and hanging.

Returning to the city centre via Micklegate takes in the **AD GALLERY** at number 73. It is a co-operative of about sixteen artists, mostly with York Art College connections, who show their work in the small but well-lit gallery.

AD GALLERY, 73 MICKLEGATE, YORK. Tel: (0904) 644438. Thursday-Saturday 10-5.

York boasts an excellent photographic gallery, **IM-PRESSIONS**, situated near Clifford's Tower on Castle-gate. Group and thematic shows, specially-commissioned exhibitions, international tours and a very well stocked shop are the public face of a gallery which also runs courses and offers various facilities to aspiring photographers.

IMPRESSIONS GALLERY OF PHOTOGRAPHY, 29 CASTLEGATE, YORK. Tel: (0904) 654724. Monday-Saturday 9.30-5.30.

If satiated by York's museums, streets and beautiful Minster then a trip out to **BENINGBROUGH HALL**, approximately six miles north from the centre off the A19, will rejuvenate the senses. It is a fine National Trust property which also serves as the northern outpost of the National Portrait Gallery. Politicians, kings, aristocrats and personalities from the eighteenth century are hung in appropriate room settings among contemporary porcelain, furniture and carpets.

BENINGBROUGH HALL, YORK. Tel: (0904) 470666. Open Easter to end October. Opening times vary – telephone to check.

THE DALES

There must be millions like me who, though not Yorkshire born, feel homesick wherever we are when the Yorkshire Dales are mentioned. The area's beauty has not the obvious drama of Lakeland nor the grandeur of scale of the Highlands, but requires patient exploration to get to know its quieter pastorale. Artists from every era have responded to the limestone outcrops, drystone walls etching the lineaments of the rock beneath sheep cropped-turf, wooded ghylls, and silvery rivers and streams. With its lonely barns, huddled hamlets, narrow snaking lanes between lush verges and twisting walls, green roads climbing high to the fell tops, and wind-driven clouds shadowing the fields with moving curtains of light and shade, it is an addictive landscape.

It is one which inspired J M W Turner who, while staying with the Fawkes family in 1808 on one of his many visits to Farnley Hall near Otley, filled his sketchbooks with views of Wharfedale. Together with the subsequent watercolours, they helped to influence the appreciation of wild and remote beauty in the landscape, both in his contemporaries and succeeeding generations. Other eighteenth and nineteenth century artists followed on sketching tours, which also took in the Lakes and North Wales. The Yorkshire painters who espoused Impressionism, such as Bertram Priestman and Stanley Royle, are fondly remembered, and the atmospheric records of their response to the Dales landscape are still deservedly popular in collections throughout the country.

In some significant ways we owe our love of landscape to artists who have furthered the nineteenth century Romantic tradition of response to place. Present-day artists, particularly those born and living in Yorkshire, continue to stimulate our looking with the passion of their seeing.

Local art club shows are full of pictures of the Dales, which, whilst often lacking in skill and plebeian in expression, nevertheless reflect a real delight in and identification with their locale. In the absence of many good galleries to visit on a tour of the Dales, a visit to such an amateur show will sometimes reward with a painting of deep feeling and unmistakeable truth to the nature of the landscape.

For the serious art lover abroad in North Yorkshire, there are few opportunities to picture-gaze, but any of the following galleries provide a good excuse to traverse the landscape – if one were needed.

Whether travelling north from Keighley or Ilkley to Settle, Skipton is on the way and proclaims itself the 'Gateway to the Dales'. It makes a happy coffee stop, the castle is one of the best I know to take children round, the market seems to be there on most days of the week, and there are attractive alleyways and canal-side walks to explore.

Settle offers rich browsing for the antiques collector, the buyer of woollens and walking gear, and anyone with an eye for vernacular architecture. A bypass now takes traffic speeding on its way to the Lake District, and the town is left to its residents, walkers, cyclists, would-be travellers on the magnificent Settle-Carlisle Railway and day trippers from the conurbations of West Yorkshire. The A65 north of Settle passes through magnificent limestone country and the village of Ingleton is the favoured base for potholers. The historic towns of Middleham, Leyburn, Bedale, Thirsk and Helmsley are also sprinkled with castles and churches, which tell tales of feuds from the Wars of the Roses, incursions by the Scots, Roundheads and Cavaliers, and long-pedigreed families whose names still mean something to local people. It is in this region that one becomes most aware of the wool and agriculture which provided the wealth in depth to build and support Yorkshire's great monastic houses and ruling clans – the same wool that caused massive changes in the industrial towns further south.

Artistically, Skipton is less favoured than one might expect. Tastes run to the more traditional representations of local landscapes and life. However, Settle has been more fortunate. Just off the main street, a sign leads visitors into a narrow yard, up a short flight of steps and into what was once a hayloft. The **LINTON COURT GALLERY** was established eleven years ago, and has pursued a policy of showing work by both young contemporary artists and well-established painters and craftspeople. Though there is often a strong regional bias, national figures with local connections – such as Norman Adams RA – regularly exhibit. Whoever the exhibitor, standards are always high, and a stock of modestly-priced etchings and smaller pictures provide a happy hunting ground for an impulsive purchase.

LINTON COURT GALLERY, DUKE STREET, SETTLE. Tel: (0729) 822695. April to end of September: Tuesday, Friday, Saturday 11-5, Sunday 2-5. During winter: Saturday 11-4 and Sunday 2-4 only.

The Linton Court Gallery in Settle.

INGLETON COMMUNITY ARTS CENTRE, INGLETON. Tel: (05242) 41701. Easter – end of September: Weekdays 10-5, Saturdays and Sundays 2-5. Winter: Weekdays 10-4, Saturdays and Sundays 2-4.30. Excellent disabled access and disabled toilets very nearby. Shop.

Eleven miles further north on the A65 from Settle, and almost in Cumbria, is Ingleton, where, in the **COM-MUNITY CENTRE**, an art gallery and arts centre has been established. Throughout the year, but particularly from Easter to the end of September, there is a varied programme of exhibitions. Ranging from first class touring shows of major twentieth century European artists, fine local artists and craftspeople, photography and exhibitions on ecology, the programme not only offers visitors a wet weather activity but also brings art to the rural community.

The road up the Wharfe Valley from Addingham follows the river for almost twenty miles before veering east at Buckden to climb over into Wensleydale. From the road, the glint of water is never far away. Sometimes the valley opens suddenly into brief vistas – small-scale excitements but wonderfully rewarding. Gradually the horizon lifts to fill half your gaze as the valley deepens and narrows. After Kilnsey and before Kettlewell, look out for the sign to Arncliffe on your left at a bend in the road. You are now in Littondale, in the valley of the Skirfare – 'flashing stream' to the Vikings – and Arncliffe was the setting for Charles Kingsley's *The Water-Babies*. Cross the river in Arncliffe and carry on another two and a half miles to the hamlet of Litton. There on the footpath to the river you will find the **LITTLE GALLERY AND STUDIO** of Ron and Margaret Walker. Their own work is on display – inscribed calligraphic plates, portrait busts and a variety of other nicely-modelled subjects and ceramics. Upstairs they hold exhibitions by local or regional artists, mostly but not all landscapes in a variety of media. You won't find anything avant-garde, but you will find honest quality displayed well in a simple, unpretentious setting.

THE LITTLE GALLERY, LITTON, nr SKIPTON. Tel: (0756) 770284. 10.30-5, Thursday to Sunday inclusive. Seasonal variations – ring to check.

Further north in Wensleydale lies the small market town of Leyburn. The same B6160, bearing right in Buckden, will take you over into one of the loveliest and least-known dales, Bishopdale, which then joins the valley of the River Ure, better known as Wensleydale, below the famous Aysgarth Falls. In Leyburn, in the small square at the west end of the market place, is the **CHANDLER GALLERY**. The permanent stock is mainly of original prints, but upstairs above the artists' materials and crafts is a gallery where changing exhibitions by local and regional artists are held.

CHANDLER GALLERY, 8 COMMERCIAL SQUARE, LEYBURN. Tel: (0969) 23676. Monday, Tuesday, Thursday, Friday and Saturday 9.30-5, Wednesday (Easter to Christmas) 9.30-12.30, Sunday (July and August) 11-4.

South of Leyburn on the A6108 to Ripon lies Middleham, a jewel of a small market town with a spectacular ruined castle which has one of the biggest Norman keeps in England. At the **OLD SCHOOL ARTS WORKSHOP**, opposite the castle, popular courses on art and crafts run from March to December, and a gallery hosts exhibitions by local artists.

OLD SCHOOL ARTS WORKSHOP, MIDDLEHAM, nr LEYBURN. Tel: (0969) 23056. Phone for exhibition dates and opening times. Bookshop. Refreshments.

If non-contemporary art also interests you and you are acquainted with the deserved reputations of such Yorkshire painters as Reginald Brundrit, Bertram Priestman and Fred

Middleham's Old School Arts Workshop.

THORNTON GALLERY, SNAPE, BEDALE. Tel: (0677) 70318. During exhibitions, 11-5 daily including Sundays. Ring to check.

Lawson, then a call at the **THORNTON GALLERY**, at Snape near Bedale, will be worthwhile. Bedale is a charming place to pause on your way east, crossing the A1 (here the Roman road of Dere Street) to Thirsk – now known (somewhat irritatingly) as 'James Herriot Country'.

Part of the main gallery downstairs at the Look Gallery, Helmsley.

In Thirsk, 150 yards down Kirkgate (which not surprisingly leads to the fine fifteenth century church of St Mary), is the **ZILLAH BELL GALLERY**. The gallery shows a wide range of work, principally painting but also sculpture, glass, metal and ceramics by regionally and nationally known artists. The small interconnecting rooms are beautifully lit and very professionally hung and managed. Interesting cards and a few quality books are also for sale.

ZILLAH BELL, 15 KIRKGATE, THIRSK. Tel: (0845) 522479. Monday-Saturday 10-5.30, Sunday 2-5.

East of Thirsk, the rising ground of the Hambleton and Cleveland Hills mark the boundary of the empty, heather-covered upland fastness of the North Yorkshire Moors. The A170 from Thirsk to Scarborough skirts the southern edge of the moors, bending to cross the River Rye at Helmsley. The attractions of this area would fill a week of any holiday: Rievaulx Abbey, Duncombe Park, Nunnington Hall and the mecca for lovers of Laurence Sterne – Shandy Hall in Coxwold – are all within a few miles. The **LOOK GALLERY** in Helmsley is close by the ruined castle. Here a very high standard of work by predominantly Northern artists, along with good local crafts, is shown in a constantly changing exhibition, with occasional one-person shows by featured artists in the upper gallery.

LOOK GALLERY, 20 CASTLEGATE, HELMSLEY. Tel: (0439) 70545. Monday-Saturday 10.30-5, Sunday 2-5.

THE COLNE AND CALDER VALLEYS

The trans-Pennine motorway from Liverpool to Hull, the M62, snakes its way through some of the grandest, wildest upland scenery in the country – Yorkshire folk would say the world. Those intent on doing the journey as quickly as possible will only glance across heather-covered moors, bleak dark-stoned fells and sudden vistas of towns below, and merely register their names. Yet even as they pass the junctions off to places such as Brighouse or Huddersfield, they will be aware of how accessible such natural beauty is to the millions of people who live in the region.

Mill towns are of necessity sited in valleys where the abundance of water powered the first looms. They then spread downstream to the river valley bottoms to be accessible to coal from canal barges as steam took over, and larger mills and weaving sheds were built. A prime example of this industrial history is Hebden Bridge, where the remains of long-silent water-powered mills can be found in the wooded 'cloughs' – often just the massive chimney bases and masonry of holding ponds are all that is left. Hebden Bridge has become that modern phenomena of the nostalgia and leisure boom of the late twentieth century – a heritage tourist town. Its marvellous weaving sheds, with their angled roof windows aligned to the unchanging north light, have many new uses, and gift and craft shops serve the regular influx of visitors. The local image of Hebden Bridge as a place of 'brown rice and sandals' – reflecting the odd attraction the town has had for New Age-type settlers in recent years – can obscure its ancient roots. These can best be recovered by climbing the hill to the village of Heptonstall above, with its rows of handloom weavers' cottages, ancient ruined church, octagonal Methodist chapel and steep streets.

Nearby Halifax lines the valley of the Hebble and climbs the surrounding hills. Once the chief centre of clothing manufacture and carpets, like so many of its neighbours it has had to find new industries and new initiatives to recover the prosperity of former days. Halifax contains many architectural gems, and the Piece Hall – built in 1779 and where

*Mossy Glen by Atkinson Grimshaw in
the Smith Art Gallery, Brighouse.*

cloth makers once displayed their wares on market days – would, if it were anywhere else, be a nationally-acclaimed architectural treasure. It now houses an art gallery and many craft shops, but the building itself competes as star attraction. Insensitive 1960s development has ruined parts of many towns in the region, but Halifax has been fortunate or perceptive enough to preserve much of the best of the past and link it with modern developments of the kind that wins the praises of Prince Charles.

Between Halifax and Huddersfield lies Brighouse, still dotted with chimneys, where the Smith Art Gallery is the result of the gift of Alderman William Smith, who founded it with his collection of Victorian paintings – another example of local patronage on a scale we can hardly credit now.

Figure Study II *(1945-6) by Francis Bacon, one of the first of his works to enter a public collection, was presented to Batley Art Gallery by the Contemporary Art Society in 1952.*

Over the hills is their neighbour Huddersfield, beset with a similar historical legacy, yet with the same gritty energy which will determine its survival and regeneration. Here the art gallery is in a 1930s-style neoclassical library building surrounded by a modern shopping centre. Previous Kirklees Gallery personnel have ensured that the collection is strong and wide-ranging, though sadly, little is actually on display at any one time nowadays.

Walking through these towns, one is always aware that beyond the streets lies the most varied walking country in England, and the natural beauty accented by signs of man's industry has made it an artistic subject for many generations. Television discovered the delights of the Holme Valley, and gave Holmfirth the accolade of becoming nationally known as the centre of the *Last Of The Summer Wine* country. Once busy with wool it is now busy with coach parties, but hand skills are celebrated in an excellent craft gallery and the presence nearby of superb contemporary potters.

Dewsbury, Batley and Ossett can seem unprepossessing if one is merely passing through, but each offers reasons for the art lover to pause, and many fine old houses and buildings have found a new use this century as museums and galleries. To appreciate what these wooded valleys once looked like, it is best to walk on the hills above, but old houses such as Oakwell and Shibden Halls in Huddersfield and Halifax and Crow Nest Museum in Dewsbury give glimpses of a more elegant past.

The city of Wakefield has a long history, some of which can be gleaned from fragments such as the Norman foundations of the cathedral, the fourteenth century chantry chapel on the bridge over the Calder, and many fine Georgian houses. Barbara Hepworth was born here – and Henry Moore close by at Castleford – and the city's art gallery has many sculptures and drawings from them both. The collection here is remarkably rich in twentieth century art, due in part to the shrewd purchasing of one its former directors, Helen Kapp, in the 1950s.

South of Wakefield is one of the most exciting developments in recent years for the public enjoyment and appreciation of sculpture. The Yorkshire Sculpture Park takes advantage of the rolling acres of landscaped parkland surrounding Bretton Hall to site major monumental works in a perfect context. It must be one of the best free days out on offer in the North, combining lovely landscape and wonderful sculpture of all kinds, in spaces that range from wide lawns to hidden groups among trees or along old terraces. It deservedly attracts visitors from all over the world, either to view the permanently sited sculptures or to catch one of the special shows, such as the hugely successful Zimbabwean stone carvings of 1990.

The recent developments in linking the funding of art and gallery provision to education and community arts has been enthusiastically espoused throughout the region. That the arts should be for all, and not merely a middle class preserve, has filtered down from the days of mill-owning benefactions to today's organisations such as Yorkshire Art Circus in Glasshoughton. They enable ordinary people without training or experience to tell their own stories through the books they publish, and to make their own art with the encouragement and example of professional artists. Their gallery mounts changing displays by artists who work with them on a variety of projects. The growth in the number of displays concerning local working class history in industrial museums is another illustration of the same democratic thinking.

This is a wide and sweeping swathe of landscape across a region, with much to see and many aspects of history and art to consider. I hope that those who frequently travel through rather than to these towns will now linger and explore, and see what their residents have always valued and enjoyed.

BRIDGE MILL, ST GEORGE'S SQUARE, HEBDEN BRIDGE. Tel: (0422) 844559. Wednesday-Saturday 11-5.30, Monday and Tuesday closed all day.

FINEGOLD CONTEMPORARY ART, NEW OXFORD HOUSE, ALBERT STREET, HEBDEN BRIDGE. Tel: (0422) 845659. Daily 10-5.30 (closed Tuesday), Sunday 12-5.30. Full disabled access.

DEAN CLOUGH CONTEMPORARY ART GALLERY, DEAN CLOUGH, HALIFAX. Tel: (0422) 344555. Monday-Friday 9-6, Saturday 9-1. Disabled access – help on request in advance. Cafe and restaurant on site during business hours.

The Contemporary Art Gallery at Dean Clough.

Violent tales of coiners and Luddites fit uneasily with Hebden Bridge's comfortable image today. Craftspeople have been drawn to the town, though some only stay a short while and the venues and goods on sale change quite rapidly. However, at the **BRIDGE MILL WORKSHOPS** a variety of crafts are produced, and particularly good quality and value is the pottery of Jan Burgess and John Kerrane.

Also in the centre of the town is the **FINEGOLD CONTEMPORARY ART GALLERY**. In the first of two rooms, a good range of contemporary ceramics, prints, cards and miscellaneous items show an eclectic taste but high standards. The rear room is used as a small exhibition space for changing shows by local and regional artists. It is a restful place for the enjoyment of good things.

Seven miles west following the Calder, the canal and the railway, one comes to Halifax. The regeneration of industrial buildings left as relics of former trades is epitomised by the Dean Clough complex of Victorian and earlier mills. Once the biggest carpet factory in the world, its spaces only briefly echoed with ghosts, because since the early 1980s it has been gradually transformed into a thriving business park, home to hundreds of small and large companies. More surprisingly, it is home to the **DEAN CLOUGH CONTEMPORARY ART GALLERY**, and the corridors are

A work by Magdalena Jetelova at the Henry Moore Sculpture Trust Studio, Halifax.

lined with items from the Dean Clough Collection of original works by regionally and nationally-admired artists. The gallery has a sequence of shows throughout the year by a wide range of contemporary artists in all media. The entrepreneur Ernest Hall, who made it all possible, has also encouraged the presence on the site of art organisations among the businesses, and the **HENRY MOORE SCULP-TURE TRUST STUDIO** occupies a lofty and interesting space. Here, internationally-respected sculptors are invited to work for many weeks at a time, and the site-specific works which result are then open to the viewing public.

Back in the heart of Halifax, the magnificent colonnaded Piece Hall, enclosing over 10,000 square yards of market space, still echoes to the sounds of buying and selling as it did in the eighteenth century. Around the sides on its

THE HENRY MOORE SCULPTURE TRUST STUDIO, DEAN CLOUGH, HALIFAX. Tel: (0532) 478249 or (0422) 320250. During each project, open Tuesday-Sunday 12-4. Arrangements can be made for viewing outside these times by ringing one of the numbers above. Disabled access available.

DAVID HOLMES CERAMICS, UNIT 53, PIECE HALL, HALIFAX. Tel: (0422) 833864. Wednesday-Sunday 10.30-5. Closed Monday and Tuesday.

PIECE HALL ART GALLERY, PIECE HALL, HALIFAX. Tel: (0422) 358087. Tuesday-Saturday 10-5, Sunday 2-5. Full disabled access on request. Craft shops, cafe and toilets in Piece Hall.

CALDERDALE INDUSTRIAL MUSEUM, PIECE HALL, HALIFAX. Tel: (0422) 358087. Tuesday-Saturday 10-5, Sunday and Bank Holiday Mondays 2-5. Small admission charge. Disabled access via ramp from Winding Road entrance.

SHIBDEN HALL, HALIFAX. Tel: (0422) 352246. March-November: Monday-Saturday 10-5, Sunday 12-5. February: Sunday 2-5. Closed December and January. Disabled access – help if requested. Shop. Cafe. Park.

BANKFIELD MUSEUM, BOOTHTOWN ROAD, HALIFAX. Tel: (0422) 354823. Tuesday-Saturday 10-5, Sunday 2-5. Disabled access via library entrance.

SMITH ART GALLERY, HALIFAX ROAD, BRIGHOUSE. Tel: (0422) 719222. Monday-Saturday 10-5, closed Wednesdays, Sunday 2-5. Disabled access – ramp available on request.

several floors, small shops and workshops cater for visiting trade, and on the lower side at ground floor level a small pottery and gallery has been established by **DAVID HOLMES**. He shows his own work and that of many of the North's leading potters, with the addition of groups of paintings and prints on the walls from time to time. Above, the **PIECE HALL ART GALLERY**, necessarily long and narrow due to the design of the building, is used for temporary exhibitions which vary enormously in type and scope. One month it may be a local group of craftspeople, next a photographer, a selection from Calderdale's collection of art and textiles or a show of particular interest to the town's ethnic communities. The rumble of machinery from the adjoining **CALDERDALE INDUSTRIAL MUSEUM** may tempt you to discover one of the most comprehensive and enjoyable expositions of a town's heritage I have come across.

The earliest part of **SHIBDEN HALL**, to the east of the town centre, dates from 1420. It is a gem of a place, with much in the way of period furniture and furnishings to satisfy the art lover, and an ambitious programme of educational activities means that you may find a variety of craft workshops in progress.

Climbing up the hill from Dean Clough on the A647 from Halifax to Bradford, a Renaissance-style nineteenth century villa houses the **BANKFIELD MUSEUM AND ART GALLERY**. The collections of costumes and textiles are exceptionally fine, and the changing exhibition space is devoted to touring and locally-originated shows, many of which have a bias of content towards textiles.

Halifax's near neighbour, Brighouse, has the **SMITH ART GALLERY** in a late eighteenth century house with sympathetic additions, which is the town's library. William Smith's collection of Victorian paintings, described by staff as 'middle of the road, moral to a fault and unadventurous', nevertheless offers both a challenge and an antidote to our late twentieth century assumptions about artistic values. Among the many enjoyable works are Atkinson Grimshaw's *Mossy Glen* and Marcus Stone's *Silent Pleading*.

Silent Pleading *by Marcus Stone at the
Smith Art Gallery, Brighouse.*

Huddersfield came late to notions of architectural conservation, but the splendid Grecian-style station building and St George's Square area is now restored to its former elegance. Nearby in Station Street, close to the attractively restored Victorian Byram Arcade, the popular taste for landscapes and picturesque views is catered for at the **BYRAM GALLERY**, which stocks paintings and prints mainly by local artists. At the other end of town, the **HUDDERSFIELD ART GALLERY** is located within the library building. Thematic exhibitions drawn from the Kirklees Collection, which includes major works by Francis

BYRAM GALLERY, 5-7 STATION STREET, HUDDERSFIELD Tel: (0484) 425747. Monday-Saturday 9.30-5. Cafe in nearby Byram Arcade.

HUDDERSFIELD ART GALLERY, PRINCESS ALEXANDRA WALK, HUDDERSFIELD. Tel: (0484) 513808. Monday-Friday 10-6, Saturday 10-4. Disabled access – lift.

Bacon, Harold Gilman, Frank Auerbach, Henry Moore, L S Lowry and Sonia Lawson, are well worth catching. (Kirklees has benefited greatly from donations of works by the Contemporary Art Society over the years.) Otherwise the spaces are used for temporary and touring exhibitions of contemporary art and crafts, often including one-person shows by leading local artists. The intriguing mixture of cultural minorities in the area is also well served by a programme of interest to all.

THROSTLE NEST GALLERY, OLD LINDLEY, HOLYWELL GREEN, HALIFAX. Tel: (0422) 374388. Daily 10-5.

Although its address is Halifax, the **THROSTLE NEST GALLERY** at Old Lindley is nearer to and better approached from Huddersfield via the A640 Rochdale Road, turning at the Wappy Spring public house. Here, in an almost hidden valley, the resident potter-owner Pat Kaye stocks ceramics, glass, basketry, textiles and jewellery from good Northern makers, all displayed in the old barn attached to the house.

EASTTHORPE GALLERY, HUDDERSFIELD ROAD, MIRFIELD. Tel: (0924) 497646. Monday-Saturday 11-5. Disabled access via ramps.

A few miles north-east of Huddersfield, at the western end of Mirfield on your right as you enter the town, is the **EASTTHORPE GALLERY**. Once the Church of England primary school, the building now offers studio space to young artists, workshops for the public and a changing programme of exhibitions. These may be drawn from other studio groups, solo local artists or touring shows.

The winding and wooded Holme Valley south of Huddersfield leads to Holmfirth, a small town of stone terraces perched precariously on the hillsides above the river. Here, despite the smallness of its display space, is one of the best craft galleries for miles, on the Huddersfield to Manchester through route just along from the traffic lights towards Manchester. **JEWELL AND ROBERTS** set high standards of excellence in their choice of exhibitors, and the fine contemporary ceramics, textiles and jewellery are by makers featured in Craft Council exhibitions nationally. They also show the work of local potters who reach their exacting standards. One such is Jim Robison, whose own **BOOTH HOUSE GALLERY** is situated high among the fields and drystone walls near Holmbridge, a hamlet two and a half miles from Holmfirth. As well as his own sculptural

JEWELL AND ROBERTS, 20 UPPERBRIDGE, HOLMFIRTH. Tel: (0484)686820/685110. Thursday-Saturday 10-5, Sunday 2-5. School holidays: Monday-Saturday 10-5, Sunday 2-5. Ring to check January to Easter.

BOOTH HOUSE GALLERY, 3 BOOTH HOUSE, HOLMFIRTH. Tel: (0484) 685270. Saturday and Sunday 2-5, midweek ring to confirm times.

The Throstle Nest Gallery at Old Lindley, near Huddersfield.

pieces, he shows the work of other potters, artists and craftspeople from the region. A well-stocked shopping corner sells domestic and other wares, and evening lectures and demonstrations are arranged when Jim and Liz Robison show visitors around the workshops and kiln area. Another artist who has his own studio gallery is painter Trevor Stubley at the **HART HOLES STUDIO** on Greenfield Road in Holmfirth. His work is varied in subject and media but always exciting in expression.

HART HOLES STUDIO,
GREENFIELD ROAD, HOLMFIRTH.
Tel: (0484) 682026. Ring for details
of opening times.

Two coil-built beakers (raku, 16" tall)
by David Roberts, at Jewell and Roberts
in Holmfirth.

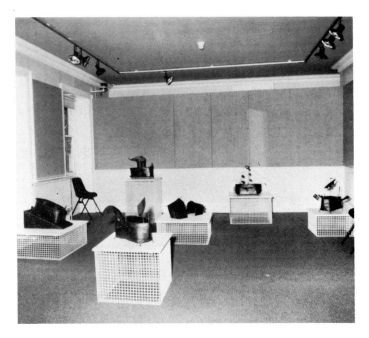

Right: Derek Horton's sculpture Taking Revenge on the Commonplace in the Eastthorpe Gallery, Mirfield.

The new exhibition space, with work by Frank Darnley, in Dewsbury Museum.

BATLEY ART GALLERY, above the library in the market place, holds exhibitions mainly by local societies, but a visit to Batley should include the **BAGSHAW MUSEUM** in Wilton Park, with its displays of Chinese ceramics, Egyptology and ethnography. Neighbouring Dewsbury has its museum at **CROW NEST PARK** – a must if you have children to amuse. Changing displays of toys and games will keep their interest, while you enjoy the classical eighteenth century mansion or one of the exhibitions drawn from the Kirklees Collection.

Ossett has the **DEARDEN GALLERY** in a handsomely restored 'shoddy' mill. The bulk of the space is given over to reproduction prints, but the upper floor has a succession of solo shows of original works and, during the summer, lively ceramics by students from Bretton Hall College.

BATLEY ART GALLERY, MARKET PLACE, BATLEY. Tel: (0924) 473141. Monday-Friday 10-6, Saturday 10-4, closed Sunday.

BAGSHAW MUSEUM, WILTON PARK, BATLEY. Tel: (0924) 472514. Monday-Saturday 10-5, Sunday 1-5.

DEWSBURY MUSEUM, CROW NEST PARK, HECKMONDWIKE ROAD, DEWSBURY. Tel: (0924) 468171. Monday-Saturday 10-5, Sunday 1-5.

DEARDEN GALLERY, DEARDEN HOUSE, VENTNOR WAY, OSSETT. Tel: (0924) 265000. Wednesday-Friday 10-5, Saturday and Sunday 11-4.

The Booth House Gallery near Holmfirth.

Henry Moore's bronze Hill Arches *(1973) in the Yorkshire Sculpture Park.*

LAWRENCE BATLEY ART CENTRE, BRETTON HALL COLLEGE, WEST BRETTON, WAKEFIELD. Tel: (0924) 830261. Open weekdays 10.30-4.30.

YORKSHIRE SCULPTURE PARK, BRETTON HALL, WEST BRETTON, WAKEFIELD. Tel: (0924) 830302. Summer 10-6 daily, winter 10-4 daily. Ring for Christmas opening times. Cafe. Shop. Excellent disabled access including special access trail.

Bretton Hall College near Wakefield, one mile from junction 38 off the M1, has the **LAWRENCE BATLEY ART CENTRE** which mounts shows by regional artists.

Contemporary and twentieth century sculpture has often been difficult for the general public to come to terms with, and the educative experience that the **YORKSHIRE SCULPTURE PARK** (next to Bretton Hall) offers is not limited to the many open air workshops and participatory events organised throughout the year. To see Henry Moore's *King and Queen* on the hillside in rain, sun or snow is to gain insight into his vision. The Bothy Garden, a lawned space enclosed by high yew hedges, offers a more intimate

Monumental Horse Without Rider
(1914-17) by Emile Antoine Bourdelle,
at the Yorkshire Sculpture Park.

setting for smaller works, which can be enjoyed in comfort from the terrace outside the very pleasant Bothy Cafe. The Bothy Gallery shows drawings and paintings by sculptors which aids understanding of their three dimensional thinking, and the Pavilion Gallery, in a corner of the garden, enables maquettes and more fragile works to be shown. A skilfully-designed access trail for the disabled, which begins near the car park, affords a rich sensory experience for all. A mixture of landscaping, planting, sculptures and natural features have been blended into a memorable but subtle statement about art and the environment. Disabled visitors can also use electric scooters to get around the park. The Sculpture Park is a surprising place, enjoyed by a huge variety of people for an even wider range of reasons.

Opposite: Lynn Chadwick's Pair of Walking Figures (bronze 1977) in the Yorkshire Sculpture Park.

In Wakefield itself, **WAKEFIELD ART GALLERY** is situated in a typical Victorian town house just off the city centre. Built in 1885, it is a fine example of middle class tastes, and the ornate stonework and etched glass may distract the eye from the collection and exhibitions. Wakefield's collection is exceptional for a provincial town and includes such notable pieces as Henry Moore's *Elmwood Reclining Figure* of 1936, Barbara Hepworth's stone *Mother and Child* of 1934 and James Tissot's *On The Thames*. The collection continues to grow with important additions by leading living artists, particularly those with Yorkshire connections. Temporary touring exhibitions visit and regional artists are promoted via solo shows.

The original Elizabethan grammar school building, renamed the **ELIZABETHAN EXHIBITION GALLERY**,

WAKEFIELD ART GALLERY, WENTWORTH TERRACE, WAKEFIELD. Tel: (0924) 375402. Monday-Saturday 10.30-5, Sunday 2.30-5. Disabled access – help available by prior arrangement.

ELIZABETHAN EXHIBITION GALLERY, BROOK STREET, WAKEFIELD. Tel: (0924) 295797. During temporary exhibitions and events: Monday-Saturday 10.30-5, Sunday 2.30-5. Full disabled access.

Wakefield's Elizabethan Exhibition Gallery.

stands now like a lost soul among the markets area and bus station bustle. It is a lovely building, and visitors to the varied and excellent temporary exhibitions enjoy the tranquility its thick walls and polished wood floors engender.

Approximately eight miles north-east of Wakefield, on the Castleford road from junction 32 off the M1, Glasshoughton's name indicates the nature of the industry, apart from mining, which has despoiled the landscape. A new industry in the arts has its base here in the old school on School Lane. **YORKSHIRE ART CIRCUS** is an organisation passionately devoted to the belief that ordinary people's history has long been ignored, and that they should be given the opportunity, through working with trained professionals, of developing the ability to tell their own history and express their own creativity. Artists who work in community projects and workshops with the Art Circus have their work exhibited in the gallery. While some have training and experience, others have had their talents discovered and nurtured by the organisation, and all draw on aspects of their experiences and environment in a variety of media.

YORKSHIRE ART CIRCUS,
SCHOOL LANE,
GLASSHOUGHTON,
CASTLEFORD. Tel: (0977) 550401.
Phone for opening times. Full disabled access and toilet.

SOUTH YORKSHIRE

The proud and ancient history of South Yorkshire's towns and cities tends to be overlooked due to overwhelming images of heavy industry, pounding forges, roaring furnaces and pit heads. Evidence of another kind of past (and present) needs to be searched for. Lovely country houses, fine urban and civic architecture, Roman remains and ruined abbeys are less easy to spot than vast steelmills, huge slagheaps and acres of post-industrial dereliction. Similarly, fine art and crafts need time and patience to discover, whereas the nearest out-of-town shopping centre or multiscreen cinema complex is hard to miss.

Barnsley is well-known locally for its markets, but how many of the busy stallholders and bargain-hunters know that a market charter was granted in 1249? It is also famous for having been a grimy, smoky place even in the early eighteenth century, when its coal and iron industries were already established. The late twentieth century has seen the advent of cleaner air, though fewer jobs in the traditional industries means that the town struggles to maintain an air of optimism. The Cooper Gallery is housed in a building which has at its core the old grammar school of 1660, though the Edwardian-style exterior hides it well. Little of old Barnsley remains and its modern buildings have little to recommend them, so it is a treat to find the Cooper and enjoy its collections and changing shows. Barnsley is surrounded by some attractive and unspoilt countryside, and it is here that two other good reasons to visit the area can be found at Cawthorne.

Doncaster's Museum and Art Gallery, opened in 1964, is typical of municipal architecture of the period, but its internal layout and design serves its purpose well. Despite its modern exterior, this art gallery reminds me of the first museums and galleries I went to as a child – a bit of everything, but full of interest. Doncaster's history is in the cases and displays – fragments of its Roman past, fossil specimens from the collieries, and how coal is mined and used. Two small private galleries near the market are brave outposts of good contemporary art and craft in an area where they are like oases in a desert.

A Corner of the Artist's Room in
Paris *by Gwen John in the Graves Art
Gallery, Sheffield.*

The Ruskin Gallery in Sheffield was opened in 1985.

Moving through the landscape south to Rotherham, the rich and rolling agricultural acres are punctuated with pits and spoil heaps, as well as country parks and mansions such as the imposing Wentworth Woodhouse. Rotherham itself has a lovely fifteenth century parish church and bridge chapel, and an eighteenth century ironmaster's house in Clifton Park houses the town's museum and collections of the local Rockingham pottery. The blight of twentieth century renewal, necessary but so often ill-executed, has stripped Rotherham even of the charms it still held when I first knew the town in the early 1960s. Its claims to have an art gallery are disproved by a visit to the Brian O'Malley Art Centre, which is in fact the library, the York and Lancaster Regimental Museum and an occasional venue for local artists' shows.

Sheffield's mills and forges have produced the world's finest iron and steels for centuries, from watch springs to ships' boilers via cutlery and silver-plated tableware. There is an energy about the city which has, despite its modern problems, kept it at the forefront of innovation in many fields. A longer history of middle class affluence and commercial activity than its neighbour Rotherham, as well as a much larger population, has meant that the arts have been supported and endowed by successive generations. The public benefaction of altruistic businessmen has been noted before in this guide, and the Mappin Art Gallery in Weston Park near the university is a perfect example of such a foundation upon which a modern city's finest amenity is based. Opened in 1887 due to the philanthropic patronage of John Newton Mappin, it was badly damaged during the last war, and eventually rebuilt in neoclassical style and reopened in 1965.

Later than Mappin but in the same mould, Alderman George Graves gave his name to Sheffield's other art gallery, endowing its collection with his own acquisitions and providing the money for the building. The Graves is in the centre near Tudor Square, at the heart of the cultural life of Sheffield with the Crucible and Lyceum Theatres close by and a quiet gem of a gallery/museum – the Ruskin Gallery – just round the corner. A walk around Sheffield will enable the visitor to discover their own favourite buildings and corners – and least favourite ones too – but it is impossible not to be keenly aware of the industrial basis of this very recent city. Some of the best industrial museums in the country are situated in Sheffield, which has a long history of appreciating the importance of preserving its own past. The attentive walker, starting in the vicinity of the cathedral, will also find fragments of Georgian and Victorian architecture.

The struggle to maintain the fabric and amenity of such towns has been hard, due to the swings of economic boom and recession, and increasing urban problems common to many of our industrial areas. However, the spirit of their population and determined efforts of councils, curatorial staff and arts organisations mean that there is a laudable amount of cultural and artistic energy at work, and opportunities for local people and visitors alike to enjoy both their heritage and a lively contemporary scene.

The interior of the Cooper Gallery in Barnsley.

Only the fifteenth century tower of Barnsley's parish church of St Mary remains, the remainder being rebuilt in the last century. It is a quiet and leafy site surrounded by the hum of traffic and opposite, on Church Street, is the **COOPER GALLERY**. The building and his collection of paintings were donated by Samuel Cooper to the town in 1914, and generous donations from the Sir Michael Sadler Collection and other bequests followed. Three light and airy inter-connecting rooms allow for a variety of uses. Interesting touring shows visit, the annual South Yorkshire Open Art Exhibition attracts a high standard of entry for the selectors to chose from, and regional artists and craftspeople are often featured. If you are fortunate, there may also be a display culled from the Cooper's own collection, which includes some excellent English watercolours, fine drawings from many eras and some good genre paintings and portraits.

THE COOPER ART GALLERY, CHURCH STREET, BARNSLEY. Tel: (0226) 242905. Tuesday !-5.30, Wednesday-Saturday 10-5.30. Toilets. Partial disabled access.

CANNON HALL MUSEUM, CAWTHORNE, BARNSLEY. Tel: (0226) 790270. Tuesday-Saturday 10.30-5, Sunday 2.30-5, closed Monday. Ground floor access.

Constable's Mrs Tuder *at Cannon Hall.*

CAWTHORNE JUBILEE MUSEUM, CAWTHORNE, BARNSLEY. Enquiries to Mr Kilner, tel: (0226) 790246, or Mr Stables, tel: (0226) 791273. April-October, Saturday and Sunday 2-5, Thursdays by prior arrangement.

DONCASTER MUSEUM AND ART GALLERY, CHEQUER ROAD, DONCASTER. Tel: (0302) 734287. Sunday 2-5, Weekdays 10-5 (Friday closes at 4).

The other jewel in Barnsley's not over-endowed crown is **CANNON HALL**. Near the village of Cawthorne, approximately four miles west of Barnsley on the A635, the house was remodelled by John Carr of York between 1765 and 1804. It is a country house museum now, with the added attractions for families of a park and farm. Barnsley's history as a glassmaking centre is reflected in the comprehensive displays of glass from Roman to contemporary Scandinavian designs, via eighteenth century crystal and novelties such as the Victorian glass model of a house. Arts and Crafts furniture, period rooms, pewter and other artefacts from Libertys of London's turn of the century designers, and a good collection of English Art pottery make Cannon Hall a worthwhile day out. At present, paintings are few but include fine Constable and Lely portraits. It is hoped that eventually the William Harvey Collection of Dutch and Flemish paintings from 1610 to 1750 will be permanently on display here.

In Cawthorne, behind the church, is one of Yorkshire's oddest and most charming museums – the **CAWTHORNE VICTORIA JUBILEE MUSEUM**. It was built in 1889 by workmen from the Cannon Hall estate to designs by the-then owner Sir Walter Stanhope, to house a collection which had been displayed in an old cottage on the site for some years. Many of the items were donated by John Ruskin. It is an eclectic, eccentric and utterly delightful throwback to earlier, less self-conscious and unscientific modes of arranging and classifying disparate items. It is still managed and run by volunteers from the village, who have every reason to be proud of their inheritance and the way they have preserved it for all to enjoy.

Doncaster is synonymous with railways, coal, iron, engineeering and racing. Not surprisingly, its **MUSEUM AND ART GALLERY** contains a fascinating display of paintings and trophies connected to one of the racing world's premier events – the St Leger – including several J F Herrings. The rest of the permanent collection on display is not conspicuously laden with fine individual works, but there is a sufficient level of quality to provide a pleasing

Touchstone by J F Herring in the Doncaster Collection.

overview of the principle developments in European and English painting of the last 200 years. Memorable are English watercolours by de Wint, Crome and Copley, early works by Graham Sutherland and Elizabeth Blackadder, *A Child's Wonderment* by Carel Weight and a marvellous *Marble Bull* by John Skeaping. Local early nineteenth century pottery wares from Leeds, Swinton and Mexborough are well displayed, as are porcelain, glass and natural history exhibits. In this heartland of staunch county loyalties, the museum of the King's Own Yorkshire Light Infantry takes pride of place on the ground floor. The atmosphere is pleasant, and the impression lingers that it is a well-used and valued art gallery and museum.

Searching for good private galleries in the area is frustrating, but the **SOUTH YORKSHIRE ART GALLERY,** by the market, is a recent venture that deserves encouragement. In a small terrace house, the owner is showing works in a variety of media by local artists, mostly in traditional style but with an eye for what is true,

SOUTH YORKSHIRE ART GALLERY, 52 COPLEY ROAD, DONCASTER. Tel: (0302) 329332. Tuesday, Wednesday, Friday and Saturday 10-4, Thursday 10-1. Closed Sunday and Monday. Phone for appointment at other times.

The displays of English silver in Clifton Park Museum, Rotherham.

CONTEMPORARY CRAFTS, 13
COPLEY ROAD, DONCASTER.
Tel: (0302) 327683. Tuesday-
Saturday 9.30-5.

expressive and skilled. On the same road, nearer to the market, **CONTEMPORARY CRAFTS** stocks ceramics, studio glass, jewellery and basketry by leading makers from all over the country, including many from Yorkshire. The space and therefore the stock is limited, but everything shows evidence of discrimination and quality.

Whilst it is possible to spend a fruitful day in and around Rotherham enjoying buildings and remains of historical interest and beauty, I could find only one venue to recommend to art lovers. **CLIFTON HOUSE**, like Cannon Hall, was designed by John Carr and began life in 1783 when it was built for Joshua Walker – famous for the manufacture of cannons and a son of the ironmaster Samuel

CLIFTON PARK MUSEUM,
CLIFTON LANE, ROTHERHAM.
Tel: (0709) 382121. Monday-Saturday
10-5, closed Friday, Sunday 2.30-5.
Disabled access to ground floor only.

Walker. As the town grew, it encroached on what must once have been an elevated, green and pleasant site – a fate that befell many fine ironmasters' houses in the region. The attractive park around it was taken over by the corporation in 1891, and the house became the town's museum in 1893. The collection of richly-decorated Rockingham Pottery is outstanding, and about four miles north at the village of Swinton can be seen the remains of a Rockingham kiln. Clifton Park is a popular recreation space for the towns-people with a paddling pool and gardens, and the house is cool and quiet for the proper appreciation of its treasures. As well as the pottery, there are displays of English glass and silver, and British oil paintings and watercolours.

It is advisable to start in the centre of Sheffield and work your way outwards on foot or by public transport, since traffic is heavy and parking difficult. The **GRAVES ART GALLERY** is on the top floor of the library, near to the Crucible and Lyceum Theatres and only a short walk from the Pond Street bus station. The Graves's collection is wide-ranging and of high quality, and the staff have a policy of creating thematic exhibitions which focus on different aspects of their holdings, enabling the public to see a larger proportion of their possessions than is often the case. Prints, drawings, watercolours (including some memorable Cot-mans), British and European paintings, and Oriental and tribal art offer a wide selection to chose from. The superb Grice Collection of ivories is permanently on show. A particular favourite which frequently gets an airing is Gwen John's lovely *A Corner Of The Artist's Room In Paris*. The Graves also shows the work of the city's contemporary artists, and initiates and receives touring exhibitions. A good cafe offers respite and refreshment.

A short stroll brings you to the **RUSKIN GALLERY** on Norfolk Street, which was opened in 1985 in what had been a wine merchant's premises. John Ruskin, the influential Victorian social and art theorist and critic, set up the Guild of St George in 1871 to curate his collection of minerals, drawings, prints, watercolours, illuminated manuscripts and plaster casts of architectural details, which he believed

GRAVES ART GALLERY, SURREY STREET, SHEFFIELD. Tel: (0742) 734781. Monday-Saturday 10-6. Cafe 10-5. Lift to top floor. Toilets.

THE RUSKIN GALLERY AND RUSKIN CRAFT GALLERY, 101 NORFOLK STREET, SHEFFIELD. Tel: (0742) 735299. Monday-Friday 10-6, Saturday 10-5. Partial disabled access. Toilets.

The Ruskin Gallery in Sheffield, with a staircase and balustrade forged by Guisseppe Lund.

would awaken in working men the love and understanding of 'what is lovely in the life of nature and heroic in the life of men'. His visionary theories of the links between types of social organisation and the production of art are still debated by contemporary artists.

Local craftspeople were involved in providing the display cases, iron grilles and balustrades, stained glass, and fine lettering on the slate slabs at the entrance and the quotes from Ruskin that illuminate the exhibition on the ground floor. Upstairs, the mezzanine floor is used for changing

The Untitled Gallery, Sheffield

exhibitions either culled from the collection or on topics which further the understanding of Ruskin's ideas in relation to contemporary art practice. A small but beautifully organised craft gallery continues the theme of the pursuit of excellence.

Before leaving the city centre, a few minutes' walk brings you to the **UNTITLED GALLERY** (ask directions from the Graves or Ruskin staff). Over 3,000 members enjoy the darkroom facilities, classes and workshops run by this thriving photographic resource centre. Exhibitions by regional photographers frequently concentrate on local issues, but the programme is varied and always stimulating.

Close by, Yorkshire Art Space Society occupy a former buffing shop. Here, young artists rent affordable studio space and run their own gallery – the **MATILDA GALLERY**.

UNTITLED GALLERY, 1 BROWN STREET, SHEFFIELD. Tel: (0742) 725947. Monday-Saturday 11-5. Cafe. Toilets. Disabled access.

MATILDA GALLERY, YORKSHIRE ART SPACE SOCIETY, SYDNEY WORKS, MATILDA STREET, SHEFFIELD. Tel: (0742) 761769. Monday-Friday 10-4, Saturday 10-2.

As in all such co-operative studio spaces, the work ranges widely in media, style and accomplishment, but there is always a refreshing sense of commitment and energy, and a detour to take a look at what is going on there will be rewarding.

Take a bus or follow signs to the university to find the **MAPPIN ART GALLERY** in Weston Park. Part of the building is a museum, with particularly interesting displays on Sheffield's world-famous cutlery. The various spaces of the art gallery lend themselves well to changing displays from the collections, chiefly of British art, and major touring exhibitions visit. In recent years the Mappin has originated some very interesting exhibitions, which have introduced new media such as video art, and shows by leading contemporary artists. Workshops, education programmes and a cafe give the building a sense of a place actively involved with its public rather than a passive resource. The nearby boating lake, park and gardens make this an ideal focus for visits by families as well as art lovers.

It is a mystery why such a city has so little to offer in the way of private galleries showing good original, contemporary work. Just off Eccleshall Road (the A625 from the city centre) is Sharrowvale Road, near Hunters Bar. Here the **ORA GALLERY** stocks pottery by Greek, British and other European potters, as well as jewellery, glass and limited edition prints.

If Sheffield's industrial past is of interest, then a visit to the tourist information office at the town hall or the Sheffield Information Service at the library (below the Graves Art Gallery) will yield detailed directions of how to get to the many industrial museums in and around the city. One of the largest, the **KELHAM ISLAND INDUSTRIAL MUSEUM**, also has an exhibition space. One of Sheffield's finest amenities is its natural setting on seven hills, which give panoramic views from many vantage points – and of course the marvellous surrounding countryside of moors and valleys, particularly in neighbouring Derbyshire.

MAPPIN ART GALLERY, WESTON PARK, SHEFFIELD. Tel: (0742) 726281. Tuesday-Saturday 10-5, Sunday 2-5. Cafe. Toilets. Lift access.

ORA GALLERY, 239 SHARROWVALE ROAD, SHEFFIELD. Tel: (0742) 661444. Monday-Saturday 10-5.30, extended hours at Christmas.

KELHAM ISLAND INDUSTRIAL MUSEUM, off ALMA STREET, SHEFFIELD. Tel: (0742) 722106. Wednesday-Saturday 10-5, Sunday 11-5. Cafe. Shop.

MOORS, COAST AND WOLDS

Yorkshire probably contains the greatest variety of scenery and land forms of any county. The lovely upland mass of the North Yorkshire Moors was shaped and carved by the Ice Ages into hidden hollows, secretive valleys, steep scarps and gentle slopes, which reveal their beauty only to the patient explorer of minor roads or well-equipped walkers. Many travellers today are so intent on reaching the coast that they see only the slow crawl of cars and caravans ahead on the road from Pickering to Scarborough, having come north from York or east from the A1 via Thirsk and Helmsley.

The Vale of Pickering was once a vast lake, and the town's ruined castle held Richard II prisoner. The church shows evidence of Norman foundation on a Saxon site, but its greatest glory are the magnificent and famous fifteenth century wall paintings. Today the art lover will find another reason to pause in an excellent, recently opened small gallery. Pickering is typical of the area's small market towns, with its soft grey stones, pantiled roofs, river and gentle surrounding fields – dotted with sheep – and nearby moors.

One marvellous mode of travel which enables the visitor to appreciate the scenery – the North Yorkshire Moors Railway – takes the line of least resistance north from Pickering up Newton Dale to Grosmont. Planned by George Stevenson and opened in 1836, it now attracts railway buffs and families on day trips by the thousand. It takes only a little sleuthing and reading of local guides to learn the history of such villages, but knowing something of the deposits of iron ore that abounded in these hills takes the guesswork out of identifying industrial archeological remains. The road from Pickering to Grosmont also offers stunning views and a variety of scenery – waves of heather and succeeding ridges to the west, and the North Sea eventually glimpsed to the east. A twentieth century intrusion into the landscape – and of doubtful aesthetic value or moral purpose – are the Fylingdales 'golf balls', but the turn to Grosmont leaves them behind and you descend quickly into a green hollow and valley where the River Esk gurgles on its way to Whitby, steam trains hiss and – a peculiarly modern irony – cars bring visitors

Fisherfolk, Coffee-House Corner *by*
Frank Meadow Sutcliffe.

to ride on the trains. A gallery here is unexpected, but Grosmont's history has encompassed many changes of fortune – it is hard to imagine it as a foundry site, for example.

On then to Whitby, synonymous with jet, whaling, Captain Cook and Caedmon, author of the first known poem in English literature. The most wonderfully-sited ruined abbey of St Hilda stands on the windswept heights, aloof from the crying gulls, fish and chip shops and crowded pavements below. A bright winter day, when smoke from red-roofed houses curls straight up into the air just as in the days when Victorian local photographer Frank Meadow Sutcliffe recorded the daily life of his town, is the best time to visit Whitby. Then its present quaintness and past history mingle unselfconsciously, without the teeming audience of summer. Sutcliffe's photographs are still reproduced and sold as postcards and prints, and the town's Pannett Art Gallery has a collection of topographical watercolours and sea scenes. Just up the coast is Staithes, a fishing village once home to the Staithes group of painters founded by Harold and Laura Knight before Cornwall's milder shores and cliffs beckoned.

The interest and beauty of the villages and beaches along the North Yorkshire coast – such as Robin Hood's Bay and Runswick – the birdlife and magnificent coastal walks fail, perhaps fortunately, to bring the crowds who throng to Scarborough. Anne Brontë is buried here, the Germans shelled it, the Romans, Normans and Saxons in turn settled here. Pirates and fishermen sailed the coast, and spa water was 'discovered' in the late seventeenth century. But it is as a 'bucket-and-spade' summer resort that Scarborough is famous. Every Yorkshire person has memories of day trips or holidays in Scarborough, and their affectionate pride is justified. The arts are well represented if a more reflective visit is desired away from the candy floss and bracing breezes.

A detour to Great Ayton, almost but not quite in Cleveland, and on your way to Middlesbrough, takes another scenic route from Whitby west over the moors. Here a small gallery adds pleasure to a stroll around an attractive and historic village.

Do not be deterred from a visit to Middlesbrough by its image of heavy industry and Teesside chemical works. Although no longer 'officially' in Yorkshire but in the bureaucrat's invention of Cleveland, its galleries are well worth visiting. If you have no wish to speed south again on the A19 from Teesside, then the round trip may be completed by returning to Great Ayton and taking the A173 to Stokesley and then turning on to the B1257 at Great Broughton, signed to Helmsley.

This is one of the loveliest routes over the moors, via a high shallow valley which eventually drops down to the River Rye. Here is my personal favourite of all Yorkshire's fine monastic ruins, the Cistercian Abbey of Rievaulx. Founded on the golden fleece of North Yorkshire's sheep, and built as much to celebrate wealth and power as the glory of God, it is a most graceful ruin in a beautiful valley.

Travelling south down the Yorkshire coast brings us into the old East Riding of Yorkshire, and firstly to the gently rolling Wolds, a landscape of rich brown soils and long vistas of arable fields in many hues. Beverley is still largely surrounded by open pastures, so that the traffic hazard is as likely to be cows as cars on the approaches to the town. Its marvellous Minster raises its Gothic bulk above the bustling market town, which still shows traces of its medieval origins in its streets and buildings. A bypass and the recent pedestrianisation of much of the centre makes it a welcome stopping place which may well delay your arrival in Hull, eight miles to the south.

The designation of 'Humberside' is still the source of debate which may eventually result in Hull returning officially to Yorkshire, though some Yorkshire patriots claim it never left. The Old Town area of Hull is one of Yorkshire's least publicised and most fascinating places for those prepared to potter on foot who have an interest in architecture, history, and in particular, maritime history. The scent of the sea in the wind is a constant reminder that the docks and Humber estuary are close at hand. Beyond is Holderness and the strangely beautiful desolation of Spurn Point jutting out into the North Sea, a windswept haven for seabirds.

GREEN MAN GALLERY, THE OLD DRILL HALL, SOUTHGATE, PICKERING. Tel: (0751) 72380. Daily 11-5, closed Wednesday and Sunday.

Entering Pickering from the west on the A170, look for a square green hanging sign above a whitewashed building on your right before the lights. The **GREEN MAN GALLERY** takes as its sign and name the pagan symbol of rebirth, an optimistic start for a brave enterprise. The owners show good original paintings, drawings and limited edition artists' prints in the two downstairs rooms, all of interesting and expressive quality by regional artists. They feature potters equally and the range of pots is good, from small decorative items to large vessels, all by well-known

A corner of the Green Man Gallery in Pickering.

potters, some of whom are members of the Northern Potters Association – a sure sign of high standards.

Many visitors are drawn to Pickering by the unique and marvellous fifteenth century wall paintings in the fine parish church, in the centre of the town. They are barely equalled by any in the country in their extent, drama and colour, and are definitely not to be missed, however pressed for time. Their now anonymous artists depicted the typical subjects of such murals, which acted as Bibles for the illiterate, with amazing energy and skill, and remind us how colourful many of our ancient churches must once have been. The Beck Isle Museum of Rural Life offers information and insights into the area's history in an entertaining manner, another good reason to plan for a lengthy stop in this very attractive town.

Now for a decision: do you go straight on to Scarborough or turn north to Grosmont – and if the latter, do you go by steam train or car? Which ever way you travel, you can't miss the **GROSMONT GALLERY**, opposite the North Yorkshire Railway car park. The two resident artists show their own paintings, drawings and prints of the local landscape, display the work of local potters and sell artists' materials. The past history of the building reflects the changes in Grosmont's fortunes. It has been a builder's workshop, garage, village hall, cinema, undertakers, tailors, waggoners and rural ironworks in its time.

THE GROSMONT GALLERY, THE OLD WORKSHOP, GROSMONT, WHITBY. Tel: (0947) 85442. Daily 10-5, but phone to check in the winter. Disabled access.

From here, the drive to Whitby along the steep sides of the widening River Esk takes about twenty minutes. The art lover may like to simply enjoy the seagull's-eye views from vantage points on Westcliffe, revel in the majestic ruins and rich history of St Hilda's Abbey, or take out their own sketch pads and colours and while away an hour trying to capture the magic of the place. In the high season, the holidaying crowds make it harder to appreciate Whitby's small-scale charms, but down by the quayside the **SUT-CLIFFE GALLERY** on Flowergate is worth a visit. Frank Meadow Sutcliffe was a pioneering Victorian photographer whose affection for his adopted town shines through the hundreds of prints on sale taken from the original glass negatives. Fisher folk and sailing ships, rural scenes and local

THE SUTCLIFFE GALLERY, 1 FLOWERGATE, WHITBY. Tel: (0947) 602239. Monday-Saturday 9-5, Sunday 1-5 (winter – closed Sundays). Access – one step into ground floor, no access to upper floor.

characters are caught with a flair for composition and technical skill that made him famous in his own time, and still highly respected today.

From Flowergate, walk straight up the hill via St Hilda's Terrace to Pannett Park and the **WHITBY MUSEUM AND ART GALLERY**. It is a curious place – a pseudo-classical front stuck on to a hangar-like building – and one with little grace, despite its commanding situation over-looking the town and with a fine prospect of the abbey across the valley. The museum collection is displayed in an old-fashioned manner which in no way detracts from its interest and pleasure, dealing as it does with the usual categories plus Captain Cook and his connections with the Scoresby family. The art gallery is sadly limited to two rooms and the entrance area. Only one of the rooms was open on my visit, and it contained a collection of nineteenth century paintings by local father and daughter artists, George and Mary Weatherill. Their principal charm lies in their being a record of Whitby through the artistic sensibilities of their age. More of the permanent collection, which includes works by Constable, Turner, de Wint, Cox and Varley, is displayed when the other rooms are not given over to local amateur shows during the summer.

You can't avoid Cook in this town – nor should you – and the Captain Cook Memorial Museum, across the river on the harbourside, is situated in the house where James Cook lodged during his apprenticeship from 1746 to 1749.

Many provincial art galleries, like Scarborough's, began life as adjuncts to the local library, but the present **SCAR-BOROUGH ART GALLERY** has been housed in a converted Regency house since 1947. The elegant Crescent is a reminder of Scarborough's long-held status as a spa and a place for Yorkshire people of all classes to promenade for their health. An excellent and varied programme of temporary exhibitions by regional artists and touring shows are interspersed with items from the permanent collection. Scarborough's holdings, like so many provincial art galleries, are rich in depth and quality. Frederick Lord Leighton, a native-born Scarborough man, is represented by *Jezebel and*

WHITBY MUSEUM AND ART GALLERY, PANNETT PARK, WHITBY. Tel: (0947) 602908. May 1st to September 30th: Weekdays 9.30-5.30, Sunday 2-5. October 1st to April 30th: Monday and Tuesday 10.30-1, Wednesday to Saturday 10.30-4, Sunday 2-4. Bank Holidays: enquire. Closed Christmas and New Year. Disabled access – enquire at attendant's desk.

SCARBOROUGH ART GALLERY, THE CRESCENT, SCARBOROUGH. Tel: (0723) 374753. Spring Bank Holiday until the end of September: Tuesday-Saturday 10-1 and 2-5, Sunday 2-5. Closed Mondays except Bank Holidays. Cafe and shop. Limited access, ground floor only.

Ahab. Atkinson Grimshaw lived in Scarborough and there are fine examples of his work. The Tom Laughton Collection contains works spanning the seventeenth to the twentieth centuries, and the presence of van Dyck, Stubbs, William Etty, Matthew Smith and Ivon Hitchens indicates that a visit will be rewarding.

Next door, in the basement, is the **CRESCENT ART WORKSHOPS AND GALLERY**. This is a lively organisation which provides studio space, workshop facilities, courses and events for local practitioners and public. The gallery shows a wide range of selected exhibitors, often as part of their educational programme. The Stephen Joseph Theatre has an exhibition programme worth looking out for, and the resident artist/owner-run **CASTLE ART GALLERY** is Scarborough old town's local private gallery.

Great Ayton brings us back to Captain Cook. Unfortunately only the schoolroom remains where he did his lessons until he left for Staithes at the age of thirteen. Across the green from the Friends school is a small picture-framing shop called the **COUNTRY GALLERY**. For once the title of 'gallery', so often misused by framers, is justified – due to the eye for a good picture possessed by the owner. The works, mostly by local artists, are modest in scale and aspirations, but nevertheless have quiet integrity and artistic worth.

The Cleveland Hills are dotted with spoil heaps and other evidence of iron ore mining, one of the factors that lead to the growth of Middlesbrough from a riverside village at the beginning of the nineteenth century, to a town of 60,000 people one hundred years later. Modern Middlesbrough owes its existence to one man – Joseph Pease of Darlington, who wanted to ship coal from the Durham coalfield and needed deeper water down-river from Stockton for his docks. The opening of a branch line of the Stockton and Darlington Railway to Middlesbrough in 1830 was followed by an intense period of growth and development of industries. The first rolling mill was opened in 1841, beginning the association with heavy engineeering which made Middlesbrough's name world-famous for great bridges

THE CRESCENT ART WORKSHOP GALLERY, THE CRESCENT, SCARBOROUGH. Tel: (0723) 351461. Open Tuesday-Saturday 10-1 and 2-5 when exhibitions are on – phone to check. Down basement steps, no disabled access.

CASTLE ART GALLERY, 127 LONGWESTGATE, SCARBOROUGH. Tel: (0723) 352726. No fixed opening hours – call and ring bell or phone for appointment.

COUNTRY GALLERY, 113 HIGH GREEN, GREAT AYTON, nr MIDDLESBROUGH. Tel: (0642) 723976. Tuesday-Saturday 10-12.30 and 2-5.

and, in our own time, the rigs for oil exploration in the North Sea.

Knowing something of its history as one approaches from the south, the view from Ormesby Bank, which takes in a panorama of river, docks and industry, can be overlaid in imagination with a picture of the marshy, ill-favoured farming and fishing community of twenty-five souls in 1801. The speedy rise of Middlesbrough has been mirrored in recent decades by a sad decline in some of its principal industries, but the place has an air of determination to survive and adapt.

CLEVELAND GALLERY, VICTORIA ROAD, MIDDLESBROUGH. Tel: (0642) 225408. Noon – 7pm. Disabled access.

For art lovers intent on seeing what the town has to offer I would recommend starting at the **CLEVELAND GALLERY**, on Victoria Road, near Teesside Polytechnic. It is nationally famous for hosting the splendid International Drawing Biennale, every odd-numbered year. Prizewinning

The exhibition 'Avant-Garde British Printmaking' at the Cleveland Gallery.

drawings enter the collection, which already contains an excellent selection of contemporary British art. The exhibition programme is varied and stimulating, being either drawn from the collections, by regional artists, or touring shows from other galleries.

The **CLEVELAND CRAFTS CENTRE**, next to the bus station and only a minute's walk from the Cleveland Shopping Centre, shows crafts of all kinds from local, national and international makers. The permanent collection of pots includes examples from Rie, Cardew and Leach, all marvellously displayed for maximum enjoyment and appreciation. It is a remarkable oasis of quality set in a less than aesthetically pleasing area, and acts as a beacon for standards of craftsmanship. The history of the Studio Pottery movement can be traced via their extensive holdings, and high-quality crafts and cards can be bought in the shop.

CLEVELAND CRAFTS CENTRE, 57 GILKES STREET, MIDDLESBROUGH. Tel: (0642) 226351. Tuesday-Saturday 10-5. Disabled access.

Linthorpe pottery, which was first produced in Middlesbrough in 1879, is characterised by bright, strong colour and deep, shiny glazes. The **DORMAN MUSEUM**, on Linthorpe Road, naturally has extensive holdings of Linthorpe ware but also maintains a temporary exhibition programme and co-hosts the Drawing Biennale with the Cleveland Gallery. The Dorman's distinctive dome crowns a building which was built as a memorial to his son, who fell in the South African wars, by Sir Arthur Dorman, another of the pioneering industrialist businessmen who shaped Middlesbrough's history in the nineteenth century.

DORMAN MUSEUM, LINTHORPE ROAD, MIDDLESBROUGH. Tel: (0642) 813781. Tuesday-Saturday 10-6. Access to ground floor exhibitions only.

A little further down Linthorpe Road, towards the Cleveland Centre, **MIDDLESBROUGH ART GALLERY** prides itself on its twentieth century collection, but has a few choice Old Masters too. The programme of temporary exhibitions shows flair, there is a small sculpture court, and local and regional artists get their turn alongside major names from the contemporary international scene.

MIDDLESBROUGH ART GALLERY, 320 LINTHORPE ROAD, MIDDLESBROUGH. Tel: (0642) 247445. Tuesday-Saturday 10-2 and 2-6. Disabled access.

If your interest in Captain Cook was not satisfied in Whitby or Great Ayton, then a visit to the **CAPTAIN COOK BIRTHPLACE MUSEUM** in Marton, south of the town just off the A174, is a must. Devoted to his early life and times, there is also a small exhibition area which

CAPTAIN COOK BIRTHPLACE MUSEUM, STEWART PARK, MARTON, MIDDLESBROUGH. Tel: (0642) 311211. Tuesday-Sunday 10-5.45 (summer), 9-4 (winter). Excellent disabled access.

takes shows on loosely-connected themes – which might be antipodean anthropology, fauna and flora, or current green issues, on the occasion of your visit.

Though less celebrated than the North Yorkshire Moors and the county's rugged coastline, the Yorkshire Wolds to the south repay patient exploration and offer small-scale delights in ancient villages. Beverley, at the southern edge of the Wolds, is a good centre from which to explore the area northwards to Bridlington and east to Hornsea, both on the coast. **BURTON AGNES HALL**, six miles south of Bridlington, is a fine example of late Elizabethan architecture, full of delectable plaster and wood work, good furniture and all the treasures and grace one would expect. More surprisingly there is also a collection of modern French paintings which add interest for art lovers.

But back to Beverley. The Minster's pale limestone gleams when the light is good, and the interior can be spectacularly illuminated by natural light which reveals the grace of the nave, the elaborate Gothic canopy over Lady Eleanor Percy's tomb and the many witty medieval stone carvings which punctuate the walls. Walking from the Minster towards the heart of the town along Minster Moorgate and then Lairgate brings you to the Public Library and Heritage Centre in Champney Road. Here **BEVERLEY ART GALLERY** hosts a variety of exhibitions of local and more general interest. Between the temporary shows, a selection of the work of Beverley's most famous artistic son is shown. Fred Elwell, born in 1870, had his first picture exhibited at the Royal Academy in 1895. After studying in Lincoln and Antwerp, he eventually settled down to a lifetime of painting in his home town, living at Bar House, next to the medieval North Bar, for over forty years. The collection of his work provides a fascinating record of life in Beverley, particularly between the wars, which, while offering some charming works, also stands as an archive of a time of rapid change.

While in Beverley, don't miss such attractions as the Guildhall – the tourist information signs will lead you to it – and whilst enjoying the Georgian facades, remember that

BURTON AGNES HALL, BURTON AGNES, DRIFFIELD. Tel: (0262) 490324. 1st April-31st October: 11-5 daily. Cafe. Disabled access to gardens and first floor only, toilets.

BEVERLEY ART GALLERY, CHAMPNEY ROAD, BEVERLEY. Tel: (0482) 867108 (library). Open Monday, Tuesday, Wednesday and Friday, 10-12.30 and 2-5, Thursday 10-12, Saturday 10-12 and 1-4.

many hide much older timber structures behind their mellow brick. On the north side of the market square, a deep-red brick building that looks as though it should be a Nonconformist chapel is in fact the Picture Playhouse, believed to be the oldest working cinema in the country. From here the spire of St Mary's Church draws the walker up to the top of Ladygate, where the **LADYGATE GALLERY** occupies the corner site. It stocks a pleasing selection of prints and watercolours, many by local artists of nearby scenes, and a good range of contemporary ceramics, craft jewellery and cards. Although not pushing the boundaries of taste beyond the accessible and decorative, the good standard of competence and professionalism results in some fresh and attractive works.

Maritime connections make it appropriate to include Hull in this chapter, though its position isolates it from the other coastal towns and the main cities of the county. Approaching Hull from the west along the M62, the first intimation of the proximity of the sea is a glimpse of the graceful Humber Bridge spanning the wide river as it turns into a tidal estuary. Dockside cranes mingle with the city skyline from whichever direction one enters, though, if driving, the one-way system and traffic thundering through to the docks needs all your attention. Follow signs for the Old Town, and park and walk as soon as possible.

Queen Victoria Square is a good starting point for enjoying the many fine buildings, museums, art gallery, docks, old inns and streets. These are detailed in an excellent leaflet called *A Walk Round The Old Town of Hull* available at the tourist information office, opposite the **FERENS ART GALLERY**. The gallery's rather austere neoclassical facade conceals elegant, well-lit galleries which have recently been extended to the side and rear by a very well planned series of new exhibition rooms. T R Ferens, a philanthropic Hull businessman, gave the money for the collection and building of the gallery which bears his name between 1905 and 1927, when it opened.

That early investment, coupled with shrewd and informed judgement over the years, means that the Ferens Collection

LADYGATE GALLERY, LADYGATE, BEVERLEY. Tel: (0482) 869715. Open Monday-Saturday 10-5, closed Thursdays except during December. Limited disabled access – ground floor only.

FERENS ART GALLERY, QUEEN VICTORIA SQUARE, HULL. Tel: (0482) 593912. Open Monday-Saturday 10-5, Sunday 1.30-4.30. Disabled access, toilets. Restaurant. Shop.

*The recently refurbished gallery 5 in the
Ferens Art Gallery, Hull.*

is rich in quality and depth. It has particular strengths in its
holdings of seventeenth century Dutch paintings and
portraits throughout the ages. These interests coincide in
one of their most popular and famous possessions – the very
winsome *Portrait of a Young Woman* by Frans Hals. Arthur
Devis's *Sir George and Lady Strickland in The Grounds of
Boynton Hall*, Stanley Spencer's *Patricia Preece*, Meredith
Frampton's *A Game of Patience* and a Wyndham Lewis self-
portrait will all be recognised by art lovers from reproduction. However, seeing them in the flesh is not only
illuminating, but they are also enhanced by their setting in
context with other works of the same period.

Twentieth century British art is strongly represented by
all the expected famous names, but also by lesser-known but
high-quality examples which make new insights possible due
to the freshness of the experience. Bringing us right up to

The Ferens Collection includes Frans Hals' Portrait of a Young Woman.

date, a typical Ken Kiff drawing, a strong Kossoff self-portrait and an early David Hockney will give the potential visitor an idea of the scope of what is on offer. From Early Italian to Scottish Colourists, the Ferens offers a quality well worth travelling to see.

Live, performance or time-based art has its own custom-built space in the new extension, a feature which must be the envy of all the other municipal galleries in Yorkshire for whom coping with the demands of such media is made difficult by buildings built for Victorian paintings, not videos and 'happenings'. Edwardian and Victorian paintings are given appropriate space and setting against dark green walls, and upstairs the Royal Society of Marine Artists' diploma works are permanently on show.

Across the landing is a display of topographical works relating to the city, which range from a fourteenth century plan, via Victorian watercolours of Elizabethan houses now lost, to reminders of the terrible damage and loss of life suffered by Hull and its people during the war – seen through artist's eyes. This is the point at which, with all this fresh in your minds, you should probably start a walking tour of the Old Town area – if you can forego the temptations of the very pleasant restaurant which, appropriately, overlooks water.

INDEX